Springer Series on ETHICS, LAW, AND AGING

Series Editor

Marshall B. Kapp, JD, MPH

Director, Wright State University
Office of Geriatric Medicine and Gerontology
Wright State University, Dayton, OH

———

George H. Zimny, PhD, is Professor Emeritus, Department of Psychiatry, Saint Louis University School of Medicine. Dr. Zimny is a research psychologist and was the principal investigator for two recent national studies of guardianship of the elderly. He is currently conducting a 6-year longitudinal study of the finances of elderly wards.

George T. Grossberg, MD, is Professor and Chairman, Department of Psychiatry, Saint Louis University School of Medicine. Dr. Grossberg, a geriatric psychiatrist, is also Director of the Division for Geriatric Psychiatry and is a past president of the American Association for Geriatric Psychiatry. He is a leader in developing clinical, educational, and research programs in geriatric psychiatry.

Guardianship of the Elderly

Psychiatric and Judicial Aspects

George H. Zimny, PhD
George T. Grossberg, MD

Springer Publishing Company

Springer Publishing Company, Inc.
536 Broadway
New York, NY 10012-3955

Cover design by Margaret Dunin
Acquisitions Editor: Helvi Gold
Production Editor: T. Orrantia

01 / 3

Library of Congress Cataloging-in-Publication Data

Guardianship of the elderly : psychiatric and judicial aspects /
  George H. Zimny, George T. Grossberg, editors.
      p.   cm.
  Includes bibliographical references and index.
  ISBN 0-8261-1176-9
  1. Guardian and ward—United States.   2. Aged—Legal status, laws,
etc.—United States.   3. Capacity and disability—United States.
I. Zimny, George H.   II. Grossberg, George T.
KF553.G83   1998
346.7301′8—DC21   97-44517
                                                            CIP

Printed in the United States of America

Contents

Contents

Contributors

Fran M. Baker, MD, MPH, is Professor of Psychiatry at the University of Maryland and Director of the Research Division of Geriatric Psychiatry at the Community Institute of Behavioral Services in Baltimore, MD. She is Chair of the American Psychiatric Association Task Force on Ethnic Minority Elderly and Former Treasurer and Board Member of the American Association for Geriatric Psychiatry.

Field C. Benton now serves as a Senior Judge, sitting from time to time in various Colorado courts. Prior to his 1995 retirement, he presided in the Denver Probate Court for 13 years, dealing in part with guardianships and other protective proceedings. He is a Past President of the National College of Probate Judges.

James Brock, JD, is the Hearing Officer for the Probate Court of Fulton County, Atlanta, GA. His primary caseload consists of cases pertaining to adult guardianship matters. He serves as a lobbyist for the Council of Probate Court Judges of Georgia and served on the Georgia Senate Elder Abuse Task Force.

Gwen E. Fagala, MD, is Assistant Professor in the Department of Psychiatry at Saint Louis University School of Medicine and staff psychiatrist at the Saint Louis Veterans Affairs Medical Center working in the area of geriatric consultation-liaison psychiatry.

Jesse A. Goldner, JD, is Professor of Law, Saint Louis University School of Law and Director of the Center for Health Law Studies at Saint Louis University.

Isabella Horton Grant is Presiding Judge of the Probate Department, San Francisco Superior Court.

Donald P. Hay, MD, is Associate Professor and Vice-Chair of Clinical Programs in the Department of Psychiatry of Saint Louis University School of Medicine and a member of the Department's Division of Geriatric Psychiatry.

Linda K. Hay, PhD, is Assistant Professor in the Department of Psychiatry of Saint Louis University School of Medicine where she directs the Clinical Trials Unit.

Sally Balch Hurme, JD, is a Senior Legal Programs Specialist with Legal Counsel for the Elderly, a department of the American Association of Retired Persons, working in the areas of incapacity and surrogate decision making.

Marshall B. Kapp, JD, MPH, is Professor in the Departments of Community Health and of Psychiatry and Director, Office of Geriatric Medicine & Gerontology, Wright State University School of Medicine. He is a member of the adjunct faculty, University of Dayton School of Law. He is editor of the Journal of Ethics, Law, and Aging (Springer Publishing Company), as well as Springer's Book Series on Ethics, Law, and Aging.

John N. Kirkendall is Chief Judge of the Washtenaw County, Michigan, probate court. He writes and lectures frequently on elder law and chairs the elder law committee of the National Conference of Special Court Judges of the American Bar Association.

Mary Joy Quinn, RN, MA, is Director of Probate Court Services, San Francisco Superior Court.

Foreword

We live in an interdisciplinary and multidisciplinary world, and nowhere is this more apparent than in the area of legal guardianship of the elderly. The amount of knowledge in each of the fields affecting guardianship is so great and has multiplied so exponentially in recent years that it is simply impossible for anyone to be trained in any meaningful fashion in all or even many aspects of the area. As specialists, we become overly compartmentalized in our thinking. Thus, quite often, there is a clear need to become more informed about and to develop more sensitivity to significant issues and developments that affect the work that each of us does on a regular basis but that emerge from professional disciplines disparate from our own.

This book is a modest, but most successful, effort to collect in one place materials that will be useful for practitioners and students in disciplines that involve issues of legal incompetence of the elderly. In addition, it will provide an orientation to others who may develop or influence public policy on the intersection of law and mental health as it affects the legal status of the elderly.

The challenge of a collection of writings such as this is to navigate in an effective manner the fine line, too often crossed, between complexity and simplicity. The difficulty is one of avoiding the presentation of material in such an overly technical fashion so as to make it difficult to comprehend by an untutored reader, while at the same time being sufficiently sophisticated so as to be useful. The authors of each of the chapters have more than succeeded in meeting this challenge. The editors of the book deserve our appreciation for identifying these authors and assembling their efforts in a seamless fashion so as to create an unusually readable explanation of the entire guardianship process.

We, as readers, however, are invited to do more than merely digest the information that the authors have presented to us. The challenge is to take a critical eye to the world of the guardianship process and to act so as to ensure that its further development is in a direction that makes it as humane and as effective as it possibly can be.

> Jesse A. Goldner
> *Professor of Law, Saint Louis*
> *University School of Law and*
> *Director, Center of Health*
> *Law Studies at Saint Louis*
> *University*

Preface

This book is intended for members of disciplines and organizations that deal with elderly persons. Such disciplines include social work, gerontology, law, medicine, psychology, nursing, and finance. Organizations include the judiciary, state legislatures, social service agencies, nursing homes, and enforcement agencies. As members of these diverse disciplines and organizations work with the increasing numbers of older adults in our country, they will encounter guardianship more frequently.

An elderly person under guardianship—a ward—has been placed under guardianship because of the loss of many basic personal capabilities, such as making a reasonable decision. In addition, guardianship strips the ward of many legal rights and powers, such as signing legally binding documents. Health care providers seeking permission from a ward to perform a life saving procedure will find that the ward does not understand the reasons they give, and, even if the ward agreed to give permission, a signed permission form would not be legally acceptable nor protective. The same difficulties would be encountered by a lawyer preparing a will or a transfer of assets for a ward, by a gerontologist seeking participation of the ward in a research project, and by a social worker attempting to place the ward in a nursing home.

A basic understanding of what can occur before, during, and after guardianship can have practical value for persons dealing with the elderly. When is guardianship appropriate? Who are guardians, and what are the limits of their power and responsibility? What recourse is there if a guardian refuses a request concerning a ward? What is the power and responsibility of the court? Can guardians be changed and, if so, how?

The purpose of this book is to provide a basic explanation of guardianship of elderly persons and the process by which it takes place. The authors of the chapters in the book include geriatric psychiatrists, psychologists, attorneys, and judges. Guardianship is very complicated, with many nuances and implications, but the authors have focused in their writings on the fundamentals that underlie and define guardianship and on the major problems inherent in guardianship of the elderly.

The first chapter, written by the editors, describes guardianship as a form of surrogate management, provides a set of definitions of guardianship terms, and presents an actual, though atypical, case of guardianship of an elderly person. Chapter 2 is written by an attorney and discusses the most fundamental and defining aspect of guardianship, namely, the law. A central issue in guardianship is competence/incompetence, and in chapter 3 a geriatric psychiatrist discusses how to conduct the often difficult process of assessing competency in the elderly. It is the change from competency to incompetency that triggers consideration of guardianship, and in chapter 4 two geriatric psychiatrists and a psychologist describe conditions that can produce this change.

Guardianship is based on law but is carried out in the judicial system. Chapter 5 contains a description by a judge of the series of steps that are ordinarily taken in guardianship cases. Guardianship cases are heard by judges and hearing officers in courtrooms that are usually, but not necessarily, part of the probate court system in a state. In chapter 6, a judge describes these aspects of guardianship and also discusses the process of guardianship appeals. Chapter 7, written by a hearing officer in a probate court, discusses the often involved and difficult decisions that must be made by a judge or hearing officer in guardianship cases.

Incompetency of elderly persons can make them defenseless, thus inviting abuse. Guardianship is a form of protection against abuse, but it can also lead to abuse. Abuse and guardianship are discussed in chapter 8 by a judge and a court investigator. In chapter 9, an attorney describes monitoring of guardians by the court as a means of preventing abuse of wards after guardianship is established.

The last chapter, written by one of the editors who is a research psychologist, contains an example of an empirical research study of guardianship and a discussion of the contribution of research based recommendations to guardianship reform.

PART 1

Introduction

CHAPTER 1

Guardianship of the Elderly

George H. Zimny and
George T. Grossberg

T he size of our elderly population, particularly the very elderly, is increasing. Elderly persons who suffer the loss of their decision-making capacity and the ability to care for their person and their finances are especially vulnerable to self-neglect and abuse by others. Individuals, mainly family members, and organizations, such as state or private agencies, that are responsible for caring for elderly persons who have become incompetent have to find ways of protecting the elderly from themselves and from others. Protection usually consists of some form of surrogate management in which decisions are made by others for incompetent elderly persons.

Guardianship is one form of surrogate management. It is a legal matter that is set forth in state law (see chapter 2), and guardianship laws differ from state to state. As a result, differences exist in the terms used to describe guardianship. To facilitate the understanding of subsequent chapters in this book, guardianship terms are defined in this chapter. A real guardianship case, but not a typical one, is described in some detail in order to demonstrate terminology and to provide concrete examples of many of the topics covered by this book.

OUR AGING POPULATION

It has been well documented that major changes are occurring in the population of the United States, particularly with respect to the elderly. Cantor (1991), citing a variety of sources, stated that the "number of elderly persons has almost doubled since 1960, from nearly 17 million to a projected 51.1 million by 2020" (p. 339) and that the "most rapid growth will occur among the 85+ population, which will triple by 2020" (p. 339). Biegel and Blum (1990) pointed out some of the effects of these population changes on the condition of elderly persons. For the general population of elderly, they stated that a "consequence of the decrease in mortality has been an increase in elderly persons with chronic impairments and functional disabilities" (p. 10). They described the oldest and fastest growing cohort, those age 85 years and over, as the ones "who are at the greatest risk for chronic illness, who have the most functional dependency, and who have the greatest needs for health and social services" (p. 11).

This growing number of more impaired, more dependent, and more needy elderly persons clearly indicates that an increase will occur in the number of surrogate management arrangements by which decisions can be made for those elderly persons who are unable to make decisions for their own care. Lack of such decisional capacity makes those elderly persons vulnerable to self-neglect and to abuse by others.

Self-Neglect

The following account of a 90-year-old deaf and retired certified public accountant was provided by an elder abuse investigator (Longres, 1995).

> I went to check his room, and it was really a mess. The mattress and covers were all thrown together. The sheets looked like they were soiled and never changed. Newspapers were all over the place. Everything was in disarray. Nothing was clean and, according to his sister, he would not let anybody come up to do anything. In the six years he lived there he was never known to have a visitor. He kept his door locked at all times. One day he didn't come down for meals all day so his sister went up and pounded on the door. She was able to reach her hand in and open the door from the inside. She found him on the floor with a broken arm. He was dirty and soaked in urine (pp. 71–72).

The next case is a composite based on actual cases. Only the first paragraph of the two-page case description is given (Kryk, 1995).

Mary is 70 years old, widowed, and lives in a rural area with her sister Martha. She received an in-home psychiatric consultation to evaluate her competence to live independently with her sister, who is 76 years old. Mary was referred to a case manager in the agency on aging by an anonymous phone caller who complained that she was dumping garbage around her property. An initial social service evaluation disclosed that there was refuse outside the kitchen door and window, but the client claimed that it was her sons who discarded the garbage this way. Her bills and other mail were stacked carelessly in one place where, she said, her sons could find them when they come on their monthly visit to help her. She said that if she had better vision she would be able to pay her bills herself. Her sons had taken care of her bills on their last visit, she said, but, in fact, the statements from the utility companies showed that her payments were overdue. There was little food in the house (her sons brought food each month, she said), and what was available was mostly spoiled. Meals-on-Wheels was making deliveries on a regular basis; however, Mary and her sister appeared malnourished, leading the case manager to suspect that the women were not eating the meals that were delivered (p. 20).

Abuse by Others

"Caroline died in a New Jersey nursing home, a poor and lonely old woman with neither friends nor family around her. This was not a part of the plan she and her husband George had designed for her waning years. But, as is all too common, she lost control and became a victim of a scheme to transfer her assets to another family" (Shillingburg, 1997, p. 1). In this case, the care giver, a nurse, slowly isolated Caroline from family and friends and then took charge of Caroline's bank accounts, Social Security payments, and funds from the sale of her home. The care giver also had Caroline write a new will that excluded the original heirs and favored the care giver.

"There is a pattern, recognized by experts around the country, that is more often successful than not. An aged person becomes infirm. People are hired or volunteer to help. The elderly person becomes totally dependent on the care givers and fearful of losing the help they believe they need to live. The care giver isolates the elderly person from his or her friends and neighbors. Then the care giver takes over the finances. The elderly person is finally induced to sell valuables and eventually to write a new will" (Shillingburg, 1997, pp. 3–4).

These examples illustrate the potentially disastrous consequences that can befall elderly persons who are unable to make the decisions needed to protect them from themselves and from others. It becomes necessary, then, for someone else to make the required decisions.

SURROGATE MANAGEMENT

When an elderly person becomes unable to make, convey, and carry out decisions required for his or her personal and financial welfare, the need for surrogate decision making often arises. The most immediate and frequently used sources of potential surrogate decision makers are family members and trusted friends. Optimally, relatives and friends know an elderly person from many years of association and can be expected to have the elderly person's best interests at the forefront in making decisions for him or her.

Relatives and friends acting as surrogate decision makers often provide the necessary concern and action to enable elderly persons to continue to live safe and comfortable lives even as their decision-making capacity decreases. For other older adults, however, such persons are not available, not able, or not willing to function as surrogate decision makers. Even worse, some persons who are able and willing to serve as surrogate decision makers will make decisions in their own interests rather than in the best interests of the elderly person. This can result in physical, psychological, or financial abuse of the elderly person, as illustrated in the above examples and in the examples given in chapter 8.

When informal surrogate decision-making arrangements with family and friends cannot or should not be made, then a variety of formal surrogate management arrangements is available.

Voluntary Surrogate Management Arrangements

Surrogate management has been defined as "a formal relationship established for the purpose of allowing another person or entity to make decisions for an adult who has or expects to have significantly limited . . . mental capacity" (Gilchrist & Zimny, 1993, p. 258). Some surrogate management arrangements can be established by persons while they have the capacity in preparation for the possible advent of incapacity. Such voluntary arrangements include advance directives, such as living wills and durable powers of attorney, and other legal arrangements for property management and disposition, such as joint ownership and trust agreements (Overman, 1991).

As an example, a durable power of attorney involves the elderly person, the principal, giving another person, the agent, the power or authority to act on his or her behalf. The powers are specified in a legal document and may be very broad or very specific. No powers other than those identified are transferred to the agent (attorney in fact). The special feature of the durable power of attorney is that it endures or continues in effect when the elderly person becomes incompetent. In contrast, the nondurable power of attorney ceases to be operative when the elderly person becomes incompetent. There is a form of durable power of attorney, called springing power of attorney, that becomes effective only when a specific event or condition named in the power occurs. If incompetency of the elderly person is named as the condition, for example, then the springing power of attorney has the advantage of not giving authority to the attorney in fact until the elderly person becomes incompetent. The springing power in this example, however, has the disadvantage of requiring the person authorized to exercise it to show that the elderly person is now incompetent.

A durable power of attorney is commonly given for decisions involving financial matters. In addition, many states have provisions in their laws for decisions to be made by the agent in medical matters.

The danger with the durable power of attorney is that the power may be misused by the agent. There is no formal supervision or monitoring of the performance of the agent, and the agent has a legal document attesting that he or she has the authority to act.

Involuntary Surrogate Management Arrangements

When no advance planning has been undertaken by an elderly person and the person becomes incompetent, two surrogate management arrangements that can be established are representative payeeship and guardianship. A representative payee is a person to whom certain government benefit checks are sent rather than to the person entitled to the funds. The role of the representative payee is to use the money for the needs of the other individual. This arrangement is established by the government agency paying the benefits and is relatively easy to initiate. The principal drawback to a representative payeeship is that it is poorly monitored.

Guardianship, on the other hand, is a vastly more complicated surrogate management arrangement but, in contrast to a representative payeeship, is more carefully monitored. It can be established in the absence of any advance directives and can take precedence over certain established surrogate management arrangements such as durable power of attorney. Guardianship is a legal process determined by state law (see chapter 2) and is carried out in court (see chapter 6).

GUARDIANSHIP

It has been very roughly estimated that between 500,000 and 1,250,000 adults are under guardianship in this country (The Center for Social Gerontology, 1992, p. 77). Furthermore, thousands of new adult guardianship cases are initiated each year among the 50 states and the District of Columbia, each with its own guardianship statute. Therefore, it is critical that those persons, agencies, and institutions likely to become involved in guardianship proceedings understand not only the mechanism of guardianship but also how the imposition of a guardianship may affect the person over whom guardianship authority is sought.

Terminology

One difficulty in writing a book about guardianship is that the statutes governing guardianship are different in every state and in the District of Columbia. Various terms are used in different states to identify similar roles and procedures. For example, the phrase guardianship of the elderly is a contradiction in terms in California. In that state, guardianship is restricted to minors, whereas conservatorship is for adults.

To reduce confusion, a definition of each major guardianship term is given below. These definitions were drawn principally from Chard and Kirkendall (1990, rev 1993). For the most part, these definitions are used throughout this book. Readers can review the guardianship statute of their own state to determine the specific terms used there.

Guardianship (in general) Mechanism, established by a court after a hearing, that empowers one party to make personal or financial decisions, or both, for another.

This definition gives the general meaning of guardianship that includes both guardianship of the person and conservatorship of the estate as they are defined below. This full or complete guardianship is also called *plenary* guardianship. The context in which the term guardianship is used will indicate whether the plenary meaning including both guardianship and conservatorship or the specific meaning of guardianship of the person is intended.

Guardianship of the person Mechanism, established by a court after a hearing, that empowers one party to make personal decisions for another.

This specific definition of guardianship provides empowerment only for making personal decisions, not financial decisions.

Conservatorship of the estate Mechanism, established by a court after a hearing, that empowers one party to control the property of another person and to make financial decisions for him or her.

Conservatorship provides empowerment only for making financial decisions, not personal decisions.

Ward Person for whom a full or limited guardian and/or conservator is appointed.

Respondent Person named as the subject of a guardianship petition who is alleged to be incompetent (incapacitated) to make either some or all necessary personal and/or financial decisions.

Incompetency Incapacity to make, communicate, and carry out necessary personal and/or financial decisions.

Court In most states, guardianship cases are heard in the probate court. The nomenclature is not uniform among states. For example, New York handles these cases in the surrogate court and Pennsylvania handles them in the orphan's court.

Limited guardianship Mechanism, established by a court after a hearing, that empowers one party to make some, but not all, personal decisions for another.

Guardian A person, agency, or institution appointed by the court as a surrogate decision maker to make personal decisions for the ward.

Limited guardian A person, agency, or institution appointed by the court to make only those personal decisions for the ward specified by the court.

Coguardians Two or more persons, agencies, or institutions or a combination of persons, agencies, and institutions appointed by the court to make personal decisions for the ward.

Limited conservatorship Mechanism, established by a probate court after a hearing, that empowers one party to make some, but not all, financial decisions for another.

Conservator A person, agency, or institution appointed by the court as a surrogate decision maker to make financial decisions for the ward.

Limited conservator A person, agency, or institution appointed by the court to make only those financial decisions for the ward specified by the court.

Coconservators Two or more persons, agencies, or institutions or a combination of persons agencies or institutions appointed by the court to make financial decisions for the ward.

Guardian ad litem Person, often an attorney, appointed by the court to investigate the circumstances surrounding the request for guardianship and to make a recommendation to the court.

Estate The assets of the ward.

The assets consist of all the items of real property, such as a house or land, and of personal property, such as a car and stock, owned by the ward.

A CASE OF GUARDIANSHIP OF AN ELDERLY PERSON

As noted above, there are hundreds of thousands of adult wards in our country. As a result, it is impossible to cite one case that is representative of all guardianship cases.

Although it is certainly not typical, a recent case of guardianship of an elderly person illustrates some of the factors and events that can arise during guardianship proceedings. The case described below is real, but names and some details have been changed. It was not a typical guardianship case for several reasons: The case was heard by a jury in a state where juried guardianship cases are extremely rare; the case was contested by the respondent and required 5 days in court; and the respondent's estate was worth more than 1.5 million dollars.

The petition for full guardianship/conservatorship was filed by a social service agency with the request that the county public administrator be appointed as guardian/conservator. The respondent was an 82-year-old widow who had lived for the past 10 years in her own condominium and at the time of the petition had more than 1.5 million dollars in a trust managed by a local bank. The respondent (or one or more persons acting for her) hired an attorney in order to contest the petition.

A preliminary hearing was held at which the respondent's attorney requested that the probate judge hearing the guardianship/conservatorship petition be removed from the case. The reason given was that 17 years before the same judge had decided a case against the respondent's sister. The judge granted the petition, and the case was moved from the probate court to another court.

At the same hearing, the public administrator, whom the social service agency had requested be appointed as the guardian/conservator, stated that his office would not accept the appointment. No reason was given.

The respondent's attorney subsequently requested of the new judge that the case be heard by a jury. The request was granted. A guardianship case heard by a jury is extremely unusual in the state.

The trial on the guardianship/conservatorship petition lasted 5 days. Testimony was heard from witnesses called by the attorney for the petitioner and by the attorney for the respondent.

The attorney for the petitioner called witnesses to testify concerning the capacity of the respondent to care for herself personally and for her finances. The first witness was a social worker employed by the agency that had filed the petition. The social worker testified that the agency became involved with the respondent more than a year before because it had gotten calls from various sources indicating that the woman was in need of help in taking care of herself and her money. These calls had come from the bank where the respondent had her trust, a state agency that operated an elderly hot line, and persons in the community. The agency made its usual response to such calls, namely, sending a social worker to investigate the situation.

The social worker visited the respondent (who was not designated as a respondent at that time) in her home and was accompanied by a trust officer from the bank to provide introductions. The social worker conducted a brief psychosocial evaluation of the respondent and then visited the respondent a second time, accompanied by her agency supervisor. A highly vocal neighbor/friend of the respondent was also present. The social worker conducted a further evaluation of the respondent and, on the basis of all her findings, concluded that the respondent had a significant short-term memory deficit and was often confused and disoriented. She recommended that the respondent be evaluated by a geriatric psychiatrist and by another social service agency.

The social worker also observed that the neighbor/friend was very domineering over the respondent. The neighbor/friend subsequently acted in a number of ways to prevent contact between the agency and the respondent. The recommended evaluations were not carried out, and the agency finally decided that it was necessary to file a petition for guardianship/conservatorship in an effort to provide help and protection for the respondent.

The second witness called by the petitioner's attorney was a court-appointed geriatric psychiatrist who had evaluated the respondent. He testified that he and a social worker had completed a 2-hour evaluation of the respondent and that he had found the respondent to have significant cognitive deficits. For example, she was unable to recall when her husband died, if she had a will, and if she had given anyone power of attorney recently. He further stated that he believed the respondent needed to have a complete dementia workup as well as an evaluation of her activities of daily living. He recommended these to her, but she did not agree to have them done. Even without the results of those evaluations, he said that he could definitely state that the respondent was significantly impaired cognitively and lacked insight into the nature and extent of her disability. He concluded that the respondent was not capable of taking care of herself personally or of caring for her financial affairs.

The trust officer from the local bank that was managing the respondent's trust testified that the bank had received a letter signed by the respondent requesting that the trust be moved to another bank. The trust officer then discussed the letter with the respondent who said she was unable to remember ever sending such a letter even though she recognized her signature on the letter. The trust officer also testified that the respondent and another woman (subsequently identified as being wanted in Texas on fraud charges) came to the bank and asked to cash a check in the amount of $1,800,000. The check was signed by the respondent, but the remainder of the check was written by someone else.

The trust officer further testified that he and two other bank employees visited the respondent at her condominium. They each testified that the condominium was badly cluttered and that they had to follow a trail between piled up newspapers, unopened mail, boxes, and clothes to go from room to room. One of the employees testified that she opened the refrigerator but closed it quickly because of the stench of decaying food.

The manager of the condominium complex where the respondent lived testified that he has been the manager for the past 10 years, during which the respondent has lived in her condominium. He stated that on several occasions in recent years the respondent appeared at condominium functions dressed inappropriately, such as in her bathrobe. He also testified that her condominium had become very messy, the smell of burning toast was clearly discernable on several occasions, and the wall behind her toaster was burnt.

The respondent's niece testified that she had visited her aunt at the request of other relatives because of their concern about the respondent. The niece stated that her aunt's condominium was in disarray and that she spent hours cleaning it up, throwing away eight bags of trash. She also stated that the refrigerator was a mess.

The attorney for the respondent called four persons to testify. They were a financial advisor, the respondent's former attorney, the respondent's neighbor/friend, and the respondent.

The financial advisor testified that he believed the trust was being mismanaged by the local bank (the trust had increased in value from 1.5 to 2.4 million dollars) and should be transferred to another bank.

The respondent's former attorney testified that in his opinion the bank was not managing the respondent's trust properly. He recommended that the trust be removed from the bank and transferred to the bank where the respondent had her checking account.

The neighbor/friend of the respondent testified in a rather wild and boisterous manner. She said that the respondent was fine and had all the help she needed. The neighbor/friend stated that people were interfering with the respondent's life and should stay away from her. She indicated that there was some kind of conspiracy against the respondent.

The respondent was called to testify. On the stand, she appeared well dressed, well groomed, alert, aware of people being around her, smiling, and relaxed. Her attorney began the questioning and asked her principally general mathematical questions. She responded to those questions rather accurately. The petitioner's attorney then questioned her, asking what her address was. She gave the address of the residence where she lived prior to her 10-year stay in her present condominium. The attorney showed her the letter with her signature requesting revocation of the trust, and she said she had no memory of the letter. He asked her why she had not had dental work done on her two bad teeth, and she said she could not afford it. He pointed to her attorney and asked if she knew who he was. She said she did not. He asked if she remembered her attorney having questioned her a short time ago, and she said she did not. During her testimony, she cried briefly several times and said a few times that she is an older woman and her memory is not too good.

The verdict of the jury was that the respondent was partially incompetent to care for herself and totally incompetent to care for her finances. As a result of the verdict, the court was required to appoint a limited guardian and a full conservator for the ward. After the public administrator declined to be appointed guardian/conservator, the neighbor/friend filed a petition to be appointed guardian/conservator. In addition, an attorney who was the guardian/conservator for two other wards filed to be appointed. A hearing was held, and the judge appointed the attorney to be limited guardian and full conservator.

SUMMARY

As a result of the aging of our population, there will be more elderly persons who need to have decisions made for them to protect them from self-neglect and abuse. Guardianship is one form of surrogate decision making. Guardianship terms are defined, and a case of guardianship of the elderly is described.

REFERENCES

Biegel, D. E., & Blum, A. (1990). Introduction. In D.E. Biegel & A. Blum (Eds.), *Aging and Caregiving* (pp. 1–24). Newbury Park, CA: Sage.

Cantor, M. H. (1991). Family and community: Changing roles in an aging society. *The Gerontologist, 31*, 337–346.

Chard, L. P., & Kirkendall, J. N. (1990. Revised 1993). Guardianships and conservatorships. In *Advising the Older Client* (pp. 7-1–7-92). Ann Arbor MI: Institute of Continuing Legal Education.

Gilchrist, B. J., & Zimny, G. H. (1993). Surrogate management. In P. A. Szwabo & G. T. Grossberg (Eds.), *Problem Behaviors in Long-Term Care: Recognition, Diagnosis, and Treatment* (pp. 257–265). New York: Springer.

Kryk, V. (1995). Three case studies of elder mistreatment: Identifying ethical issues. *Journal of Elder Abuse & Neglect, 7*(2/3), 19–30.

Longres, J. F. (1995). Self-neglect among the elderly. *Journal of Elder Abuse & Neglect, 7*(1), 69–86.

Overman, W. H. (1991). Preventing elder abuse and neglect through advance legal planning. *Journal of Elder Abuse & Neglect, 3*(4), 5–21.

Shillingburg, P. (1997). Caregiver exploitation. *National Guardian, 10* (1), 1, 4.

The Center for Social Gerontology (1992). *National Study of Guardianship System and Feasibility of Implementing Expert Systems.* Final Report to U.S. Administration on Aging. Ann Arbor, MI: The Center for Social Gerontology.

CHAPTER 2

Legal Basis of Guardianship

Marshall B. Kapp

G uardianship is a legal relationship that may be authorized only by a state court (usually in the probate or equity division). This relationship is between a ward (the person whom the court has declared to be incompetent or incapacitated to make particular decisions) and a guardian (whom the court appoints as the surrogate decision maker for the ward) (Frolik & Barnes, 1992; Frolik & Brown, 1992; Strauss, Wolf, & Shilling, 1990).

Although this concept may be traced back to the ancient Roman times of Cicero, modern American guardianship law originated in English common law and a statute, *De Praerogative Regis*, dating from the reign of Edward II at the beginning of the fourteenth century (Neugebauer, 1989). This statute recognized that the sovereign was responsible for the property of any person found to be a lunatic "whose wit and memory had failed." Lunacy was determined by an inquisition and an investigation of the facts before a sworn jury composed of 12 men. The emphasis of early guardianship laws on property matters is indicated by the fact that the prerogative to make decisions for the incapacitated person originally was exercised by the Exchequer (Finance Minister) as an aspect of tax collection.

The use of guardianship to safeguard a ward's personal, including medical, well-being is of more recent vintage. The ethical justification for state (that is, legislative and judicial) imposition of a surrogate decision maker for an incapacitated individual in the realm of both personal and financial decisions is found in two fundamental and related principles. The principle of nonmaleficence instructs us to "do no harm" to others (*primum non nocere*). This is a passive command. The related precept of beneficence instructs us to help others who need assistance, to affirmatively "do good" unto others. These ethical principles have been transformed into the legal doctrine of *parens patriae* (literally, father of the land), the inherent authority and responsibility of a benevolent society to intervene, even over objection, to protect people who cannot protect themselves (Hull, Holmes, & Karst, 1990). Thus, instead of abandoning cognitively incapacitated individuals to a superficial, meaningless autonomy to make self-harmful decisions or to neglect their own basic needs, the state may exercise its authority to protect even unwilling disabled individuals from their own folly or intellectual deficits.

Every adult person is presumed to be legally competent to make individual choices in life. This presumption may be declared invalid, and a substitute decision maker may be appointed only upon a sufficient showing that the individual is mentally unable to take part in a rational decision-making process. A legal ruling of incompetence signifies that a person, because of a lack of the capacity to contemplate and weigh choices rationally, cannot care adequately for his or her own person or property.

There are basically two motives for initiating judicial appointment of a guardian for another individual. The first is altruism, a sincere desire to protect and benefit a human being who needs help. Thus, the demand for guardianship often is generated by members of the helping professions, social agencies, and private citizens (relatives or friends) who seek a workable legal method for assuming control over the personal or financial affairs of a disabled individual. Many guardianship petitions are initiated as a result of health or human service provider compliance with state elder abuse and neglect reporting requirements.

The second motivation is more pragmatic; guardianship may be sought for the primary purpose of benefiting a service provider, for example, a health care professional, nursing home, or hospital. Such providers may use the guardianship structure to definitively establish a party who is responsible for paying for services used by the ward and who is legally capable of giving binding informed consent for medical treatment.

Guardianship law represents a tension between our commitment to individual autonomy or self-determination—the right to be left alone to "do one's own thing"—on the one hand and society's commitment to *parens patriae*, built on the principles of beneficence and nonmaleficence on the other. Dedication to the autonomy principle is quite vigorous in the United

States, as reflected by the numerous substantive and procedural due process safeguards (see below) built into state guardianship statutes as intentional obstacles to the imposition of guardianship. In Great Britain, by contrast, a clear beneficence-dominated, medically oriented model vastly eases the process of guardianship imposition (Barnes, 1992).

Despite the elevation of personal autonomy to a preferred place among our ethical principles, a number of critics articulately posit that any guardianship case is inherently and unavoidably an excessive exercise in professional and familial coercion and intrusion. According to this view, benevolent motives (let alone situations where guardianship is actually sought to further a third party's agenda) will inevitably lead to paternalistic (ergo, objectionable) behavior (Frolik, 1981; Horstman, 1975; Mitchell, 1979; Schmidt, 1986).

STATE STATUTES

Guardianship historically has been a matter of state, as opposed to federal, jurisdiction. Every state has enacted statutes that empower the courts to appoint guardians for decisionally incapacitated persons. For a list of relevant state statutes, see Table 2.1.

Most state guardianship statutes are similar in content because they are based on the Uniform Probate Code (UPC), Article 5. At the same time, variations in both the letter of the law and its application do exist across the United States (Johnson, 1990), so knowledge of the specific statute in one's particular jurisdiction is imperative. These interstate variations have prompted calls for (U.S. Congress, House Select Committee on Aging, 1989), and the introduction of, federal legislation (H.R. 800, S. 352, National Guardianship Rights Act of 1991) that would compel states to enact certain minimum procedural protections for wards and proposed wards, at least where someone other than a family member is the potential or actual guardian. Such federal legislation has not yet been enacted.

Revisions and Reforms

The past decade has been a period of substantial reexamination and revision of existing state guardianship statutes on the part of many legislatures. Several states have made substantive changes in their guardianship laws by sub-

TABLE 2.1 State Statutory Authority for Guardianship

Alabama Code §§ 26-1-1 to 9-16 (1997)
Alaska Stat. §§ 13.26.005 to .410 (1997)
Arizona Rev. Stat. Ann. §§ 14-5301 to 5607 (1997)
Arkansas Stat. Ann. §§ 28-65-101 to 67-111 (1997)
California Prob. Code §§ 1400 to 3803 (1997)
Colorado Rev. Stat. §§ 15-14-301 to 432 (1997)
Connecticut Gen. Stat. Ann. §§ 45-70 to 77 (1997)
Delaware Code Ann. tit. 12 §§ 3701 to 3997 (1997)
District of Columbia Code Ann. §§ 21-2001 to 2077 (1997)
Florida Stat. Ann. §§ 744.101 to 747.531 (West 1997)
Georgia Code Ann. §§ 29-2-1 to 8-7 (1997)
Hawaii Rev. Stat. §§ 560:5-101 to 430 (1997)
Idaho Code §§ 15-5-101 to 432 (1997)
Illinois Ann. Stat. ch. 110 ½, para. 11a-1 to 22 (1997)
Indiana Code Ann. §§ 29-3-1-1 to 15 (1997)
Iowa Code Ann. §§ 633.566 to .682 (1997)
Kansas Stat. Ann. §§ 59-3001 to 3038 (1997)
Kentucky Rev. Stat. Ann. §§ 387.500 to .990 (1997)
Louisiana Civ. Code Ann. art. 389 to 426, La. Code Civ. Proc. Ann.
    art. 4541 to 4557 (1997)
Maine Rev. Stat. Ann. tit. 18A, §§ 5-101 to 432 (1997)
Maryland Est. & Trusts Code Ann. §§ 13-201 to 806 (1997)
Massachusetts Gen. Laws Ann. ch. 201, §§ 1 to 31 (1997)
Michigan Comp. Laws Ann. §§ 27.5401 to 5461 (1997)
Minnesota Stat. Ann. §§ 525.539 to .614 (1997)
Mississippi Code Ann. §§ 93-13-121 to 267 (1997)
Missouri Ann. Stat. §§ 475.010 to .340 (1997)
Nebraska Rev. Stat. §§ 30-2617 to 2661 (1997)
Nevada Rev. Stat. §§ 156.013 to .215 (1997)
New Hampshire Rev. Stat. Ann. §§ 464-A:1 to :44 (1997)
New Jersey Stat. Ann. §§ 3B:1-1 to 4:83-12 (1997)
New Mexico Stat. Ann. §§ 45-5-301 to 432 (1997)
New York Ment. Hyg. Law §§ 81.01 (1997)
North Carolina Gen. Stat. §§ 35-A-1101 to 1217 (1997)
North Dakota Cent. Code §§ 30.1-26-01 to 29-32 (1997)
Ohio Rev. Code Ann. §§ 2101.01 to .51 (1997)
Oklahoma Stat. Ann. tit. 30, §§ 1-101 to 5-101 (West 1992)

TABLE 2.1 *(Continued)*

Oregon Rev. Stat. §§ 126.003 to 126.396 (1997)
Pennsylvania 20 Pa. Cons. Stat. Ann. §§ 5501 to 5537 (1997)
Rhode Island Gen. Laws §§ 33-15-1 to 45 (1997)
South Carolina Code Ann. §§ 62-5-301 to 432 (1997)
South Dakota Codified Laws Ann. §§ 30-26-1 to 29-52 (1997)
Tennessee Code Ann. §§ 34-2-101 to 4-213 (1997)
Texas Prob. Code Ann. art. 108-1300 (1997)
Utah Code Ann. §§ 75-5-301 to 433 (1997)
Vermont Stat. Ann. tit. 14, §§ 2671 to 3081 (1997)
Virginia Code Ann. §§ 37.1-128.01 to 142 (1997)
Washington Rev. Code Ann. §§ 11.88.005 to .92.190 (1997)
West Virginia Code §§ 27-11-1 to 44-10A-6 (1997)
Wisconsin Stat. Ann. §§ 880.01 to .39 (1997)
Wyoming Stat. §§ 3-1-101 to 4-109 (1997)

stituting in place of traditional definitions of incompetence that rely heavily on diagnostic labels (e.g., the patient is depressed or demented) a reliance on more objective standards designed to focus on the individual's functional ability to manage personal care or finances on a daily basis—that is, that focus more on the person's ability to meet basic needs rather than just on his or her clinical "condition" (Wang, Burns, & Hommel, 1990).

Hence, state guardianship statutes today typically contain a two-step definition of competence (Anderer, 1990). First, the individual must fall within a specific category, such as old age, mental illness, or developmental disability. Second, the individual must be found to be impaired functionally—that is, unable to care appropriately for his or her own person or property—as a result of being within that category. Incompetence cannot be equated with the categorical condition (such as advanced years) alone, so the determination of functional, behavioral, or adaptive disability is essential.

Over the past decade, states have also enacted a variety of procedural reforms aimed at assuring potential wards greater due process protections against the unnecessary, premature, or improper loss of decisional rights. This legislative activity was largely a response to a 1987 Pulitzer Prize–winning series of articles by the Associated Press (AP) based on a nationwide survey of guardianship practices (American Bar Association,

1989). The AP found a dangerously burdened and troubled system that regularly puts elderly lives in the hands of others with little or no evidence of necessity, then fails to guard against abuse, theft, and neglect.

These state-enacted procedural reforms deal with such matters as who should perform assessments of competence, with a marked preference for the multidisciplinary and interdisciplinary perspective; the content of the assessor's report to the court; the appointment of outside visitors to supplement the formal assessment; the right to counsel as advocate; the ward's presence at the hearing; more rigorous requirements with regard to petitions; enhanced notice requirements; formalized hearing procedures and rules; and more specificity in the court's findings and in the order appointing the guardian (Hommel, Wang, & Bergman, 1990; Wood, Stiegel, Sabatino, & Edelstein, 1993). Substantial legislative reforms have also been passed in the spheres of limited and temporary guardianship.

A number of states are moving away from referring to the legal status of the ward as "incompetent" and toward the language of "decisional incapacity." This change reflects the movement in substantive standards, alluded to above, away from an emphasis on diagnostic category or label and toward a more proper emphasis on the individual's current functional abilities or deficits.

FUNCTIONS OF GUARDIANS

Judicial appointment of a guardian to make decisions on behalf of a person who has been adjudicated incompetent or incapacitated means that the ward no longer retains the legal power to exercise those decisional rights that have been delegated by the court to the guardian. The legal system historically has treated guardianship as an all-or-nothing proposition, with global findings of incompetence accompanied by virtually complete disenfranchisement of the ward. Plenary guardians ordinarily are awarded total power to control the ward's finances, to make decisions about where and with whom the ward will live, and to grant or withhold authorization for diagnostic or therapeutic interventions for, or biomedical or behavioral research on, the ward. Guardianships have frequently been used, for example, as a backdoor means of nursing home placement since, unlike the situation for public mental institutions, no procedural barriers stand in the way of a "voluntary admission" to a nursing home by a guardian.

The trend lately, however, has been toward statutory recognition of the concept of limited or partial guardianship that accounts for the decision-specific, waxing and waning nature of mental capacity for many persons and the ability of some people to rationally make certain kinds of choices but not others and encouragement of judicial deference to this concept. State statutes also have been widely amended recently to permit judges to grant guardianship on a temporary, time-limited basis, rather than the prevalent indefinite orders that shift the burden of proof regarding regained capacity onto the ward.

These trends reflect legislative deference to the least restrictive alternative (LRA), sometimes called the least intrusive alternative, principle concerning state impingement of an individual's rights to personal autonomy. The LRA principle is a well-established tenet of American constitutional law, incorporated in the Fourteenth Amendment's due process protections for liberty, and is predicated on the ethical notions of autonomy, nonmaleficence, and beneficence. Petitioners are now expected to explore less restrictive or intrusive alternatives to guardianship prior to initiating formal proceedings (Kapp & Detzel, 1992).

Under limited, partial, or temporary guardianships, courts design their orders with the LRA principle in control, fashioning the orders to very explicitly delineate the particular and exclusive types of decisions that the ward is incapable of making and over which the guardian may exercise proxy authority, with remaining power residing with the ward (Frolik, 1990; Rosoff & Gotlieb, 1987). Limited, partial, or temporary guardianship statutes may be permissive, allowing but not requiring courts to carefully tailor the guardian's powers to the ward's needs, or they may mandate that the powers of the guardian be drawn as narrowly as possible (Jost, 1980). Even in the absence of legislation, state courts have general equity jurisdiction to create limited, partial, or temporary guardianships *sua sponte* (on their own initiative).

SUMMARY

This chapter has attempted to sketch out the basic structure that the legal system has devised over time for dealing benevolently with the reality of individuals for whom financial and personal decisions must be made but who lack the present capacity to rationally make those decisions for themselves. Subsequent chapters in this book explicate in depth the operational details and the actual impact of the guardianship system in practice.

REFERENCES

American Bar Association, Commissions on the Mentally Disabled and on Legal Problems of the Elderly. (1989). *Guardianship: An agenda for reform—recommendations of the National Guardianship Symposium and policy of the American Bar Association.* Washington, DC: American Bar Association.

Anderer, S. J. (1990). *Determining competency in guardianship proceedings.* Washington, DC: American Bar Association, Division of Public Services.

Barnes, A. P. (1992). Beyond guardianship reform: A reevaluation of autonomy and beneficence for a system of principled decision-making in long term care. *Emory Law Journal, 41*, 633–760.

Frolik, L. A. (1981). Plenary guardianship: An analysis, a critique and a proposal for reform. *Arizona Law Review, 23*, 599.

Frolik, L. A. (1990). Elder abuse and guardians of elderly incompetents. *Journal of Elder Abuse and Neglect, 2*(3/4), 31–56.

Frolik, L. A., & Barnes, A. P. (1992). *Elderlaw: Cases and materials.* Charlottesville, VA: Michie Company.

Frolik, L. A., & Brown, M. C. (1992). *Advising the elderly or disabled client.* Englewood Cliffs, NJ: Rosenfeld Launer Publications.

Hommel, P. A., Wang, L., & Bergman, J. A. (1990). Trends in guardianship reform: Implications for the medical and legal professions. *Law, Medicine & Health Care, 18*(3), 213–226.

Horstman, P. M. (1975). Protective services for the elderly: The limits of parens patriae. *Missouri Law Review, 40*, 215.

Hull, L., Holmes, G. E., & Karst, R. H. (1990). Managing guardianships of the elderly: Protection and advocacy as public policy. *Journal of Elder Abuse and Neglect, 2*(3/4), 145–162.

Johnson, T. F. (1990). Guardianship in the South: Strategies for preserving the rights of older persons. *Journal of Aging and Social Policy, 2*(1), 33–50.

Jost, T. (1980). The Illinois guardianship for disabled adults legislation of 1978 and 1979: Protecting the disabled from their zealous protectors. *Chicago-Kent Law Review, 56*, 1087.

Kapp, M. B., & Detzel, J. A. (1992). *Alternatives to guardianship for the elderly: Legal liability disincentives and impediments.* Dayton, OH: Wright State University.

Mitchell, A. M. (1979). The objects of our wisdom and our coercion: Involuntary guardianship for incompetents. *Southern California Law Review, 52*, 1405.

Neugebauer, R. (1989). Diagnosis, guardianship, and residential care of the mentally ill in medieval and early modern England. *American Journal of Psychiatry, 146*(12), 1580–1584.

Rosoff, A. J., & Gottlieb, G. L. (1987). Preserving personal autonomy for the elderly: Competency, guardianship, and Alzheimer's disease. *Journal of Legal Medicine, 8*(1), 1–47.

Schmidt, W. C. (1986). Adult protective services and the therapeutic state. *Law & Psychology Review, 10*, 101.

Strauss, P. J., Wolf, R., & Shilling, D. (1990). *Aging and the law*. Chicago: Commerce Clearing House, Inc.

U.S. Congress, House Select Committee on Aging, Subcommittee on Housing and Consumer Interests. (1989). *Model standards to ensure quality guardianship and representative payee services*. Washington, DC: U.S. Government Printing Office (Committee Pub. No. 101-729).

Wang, L., Burns, A. M., & Hommel, P. A. (1990). Trends in guardianship reform: Roles and responsibilities of legal advocates. *Clearinghouse Review, 24*(6), 561–569.

Wood, E., Stiegel, L. A., Sabatino, C. P., & Edelstein, S. (1993). Overview of 1992 State Law Changes in Guardianship, Durable Powers of Attorney, Health-Care Decisions, and Home Equity Mortgages. *Clearinghouse Review, 26*, 1277–1286.

PART 2

Psychiatric Aspects

CHAPTER 3

Assessing Competency in the Elderly

Fran M. Baker

A s noted in the previous chapter, it is incompetency of individuals and the consequent need for protection of these individuals that underlies American guardianship law and the earlier English common law upon which it is based. As will be explained in chapter 7, the adjudication or determination of competency/incompetency of individuals is the fundamental and sometimes very difficult decision that must be made by the courts. The purpose of this chapter is to answer two questions about competency within a general legal and judicial context. What is competency? How is it assessed?

WHAT IS COMPETENCY?

Before answering this question, it is necessary to determine whether competency is the proper term to use in this legal/judicial context or whether capacity should be used. The issue arises because some state guardianship laws do not use the term competency/incompetency but instead use capacity/incapacity. In Missouri law, for example, a person may be adjudicated incapacitated, but the law makes no mention of incompetency.

Kapp and Mossman (1996) provide a distinction between the two terms in the general legal/judicial context. They state that ". . . competence traditionally has referred to a formal adjudication by a court regarding an individual's legal status, whereas capacity has been used to refer more broadly to working assessments by clinicians regarding an individual's ability to make specific kinds of decisions" (p. 73). This is a reasonable distinction, but because the terms competency/incompetency are widely used, they will generally be used in this book.

The guardianship statute in each state and in the District of Columbia contains a definition or description of competency or incompetency, sometimes identified as capacity or incapacity. The statute is ordinarily quite general in its definition of competency in order to cover the wide array of types and degrees of competency that may be encountered by the courts, however. Much discretion is thus left to the judge in determining what constitutes competency in a particular case.

There is no fully agreed upon definition of competency, but two major themes are evident in the literature on the topic. One theme is the designation of capacity to make decisions as the essence of competency, and the other is the operation of functional abilities in the decision making process.

Decision Making

High (1994) states that "many practitioners, researchers, and ethicists use the term *competence* interchangeably with *decision-making capacity*" (p. 447). Kapp (1990) says that before appointing a guardian or conservator "the court must make a determination that the individual in question (the proposed ward) presently lacks the mental capacity to make decisions on his [her] own behalf" (p. 15).

If the court determines that a respondent is not able to make decisions that serve to provide for necessary basic care of self and/or care of property, then the court will appoint a substitute decision maker—a guardian and/or conservator. It then becomes the responsibility of the guardian and the conservator to make decisions, with the ward contributing to the extent possible, about the personal care of the ward and the care of the ward's assets.

Functional Abilities

Although there is rather widespread agreement that competency is essentially decision-making capacity, there is rather less agreement on what functional abilities are involved in making a decision and how to assess those abilities. Functional abilities refer to the steps or procedures that a person must be able to carry out in order to make a decision. What is involved in making a decision? High (1994) identifies ". . . the ability (1) to receive, comprehend, and understand information about his or her specific situation, (2) to deliberate on accessible alternatives and to appreciate that he or she has a choice, and (3) to make a reasoned choice, that is, to select an option and provide reasons for the choice" (p. 448). Applebaum and Grisso (1988) identify communicating choices, understanding relevant information, appreciating the situation and its consequences, and manipulating information rationally. If a person is not able to carry out one or more functions such as described by High or Applebaum and Grisso, then his or her decision-making capacity is impaired. The court must determine whether the degree of impairment warrants appointment of a guardian and, if so, whether it should be a full or limited guardianship.

Grisso (1986) identified functional abilities as covering any abilities and capabilities, including those involved in decision making, that are required in order for a person to be considered competent in particular legal contexts. "As used here, the term *functional abilities* refers to that which an individual can do or accomplish, as well as to the specific knowledge, understanding, or beliefs that may be necessary for the accomplishment" (Grisso, 1986, p. 15). For example, two quite different functions that are important to consider in guardianship and conservatorship cases are, first, knowing the steps to take to obtain protection from an imminently dangerous situation and, second, keeping track of financial expenditures. These are only two of many functional abilities in addition to decision-making ability required by a person to care for self and for finances.

The task of identifying the requisite functional abilities to be considered by the court in adjudicating competency in guardianship cases has not been accomplished to date and may never be accomplished (Kapp & Mossman, 1996). The section in this chapter on assessing competency will describe three ways of obtaining information about respondents that can be of use to the court adjudicating competency. It should be evident that the court can be faced with having to make some very complicated and difficult decisions in adjudicating competency (see chapter 7).

Competency for What?

There are a variety of legal areas in which the question of competency arises. Grisso (1986) identified six legal competencies, namely, competency to stand trial, waiver of rights to silence and legal counsel, not guilty by reason of insanity, parenting capacity (determination of child custody), guardianship and conservatorship, and competency to consent to treatment. Because of the increasing number of elderly persons in our country and the availability of improved life-sustaining technology, competency to consent to treatment is an area of widespread concern in the legal and health care fields (Applebaum & Grisso, 1988; Fitten, Lusky, & Hamann, 1990; Haddad, 1988; High, 1994; Lo, 1990).

The answer to the question of "competency for what" is important because the nature and degree of many of the functional abilities needed for competency are specific to the particular legal context. The notion that there is a single general competency has given way to the idea that a set of specific functional abilities is required in a given legal context. Determining what specific functional abilities are required for competency in a certain context is a complicated but necessary task, as noted earlier. Even within the legal context of guardianship and conservatorship, the types and degrees of functional abilities needed to care for one's personal welfare (taking medication and maintaining a safe living arrangement) are not the same as those needed to care for one's financial affairs (paying bills and investing funds). Because of the differences in these two sets of functional abilities, a respondent may be adjudicated partially incompetent for care of self, and a limited guardian appointed, but completely incompetent for care of finances, and a full conservator appointed (as was the outcome of the case described in the first chapter).

Applebaum and Grisso (1988) cited manipulating information rationally as one of the standards or functions involved in determining a person's competence to make decisions. As applied to the matter of competency to consent to treatment, "rational manipulation of information is the ability to use logical processes to compare the benefits and risks of various treatment options" (Applebaum & Grisso, 1988. p. 1636). Making a comparison involves weighing the pros and cons of each treatment option in order to make a decision about treatment. In determining competency to make the decision, it is the process of arriving at the decision rather than the decision itself that is important. Two people can express the same decision about treatment, one by a reasoned logical process and the other by a thoughtless or unreasonable selection of one of the alternatives presented. Weisensee and Kjervik (1989) cite the case of a 72-year-old woman who refused to consent to surgery on her seriously gangrenous feet, explaining that she wanted to live and to keep her feet. These two wishes were incompatible and, thus, could not logically lead to the decision to refuse treatment. A guardian was appointed and the guardian consented to the surgery for the ward.

Two other legal areas in which the issue of competency arises are testimonial and testamentary competencies. Testimonial competency refers to the capacity of an individual to testify in court. The person must be able to recount factual information and understand the nature of swearing under oath. If there is a long delay before a case reaches the court (sometimes several years), an older person who has developed a memory disorder may no longer be a reliable informant. In instances in which the abuse of cognitively impaired nursing home residents has resulted in a court case, some of the alleged victims did not possess testimonial capacity at the time that the case came to trial (Baker, Perr, & Yesavage, 1986; Lang, 1980).

Testamentary competency refers to the capacity to make a will. Three functional abilities required for testamentary capacity are knowledge that one is making a will, knowledge of the extent of one's bounty (or estate), and knowledge of the likely heirs or natural recipients of one's bounty. Some jurisdictions require that the individual be able to communicate his or her desires regarding the distribution of the estate. Although age per se does not preclude making a will, it may raise the issue of competency. A codicil is a partial, subsequent will or an addition to an existing will. A codicil recently added to a will that had been completed several years previously may be challenged on the basis of incompetence based upon age (Baker & Finkel, 1988). Although such a challenge is based on ageism, it is important to alert the older person to its existence. Some attorneys have encouraged their older clients to have a concurrent psychiatric evaluation to provide documentation of their cognitive capacity. Videotapes in which the older individual specifies the extent of his or her estate and its distribution have been used to document cognitive capacity, orientation, and judgment. Some psychiatrists have instructed their patients to see them on the day that a change in a will is being made. If a will is challenged at probate, a request for the posthumous evaluation of the older person's cognitive capacity may result (Sadoff, 1991). This retrospective assessment of the cognitive function and judgment of the deceased individual at the time that the will was prepared requires diligent effort on the part of a consulting psychiatrist to establish the cognitive capacity and judgment of the patient at the time that the will was made. The assessment is made easier with videotapes and medical records.

ASSESSING COMPETENCY

For a variety of reasons, there is no standard way of assessing competency. State statutes differ in the definition of competency. Judges in the same state do not necessarily have the same concept of competency. There are different answers to the questions of competency for what. In addition, the psychiatric disorders described in chapter 4 have an impact on the functional abilities constituting competency.

Rather than try to describe approaches to assessing the varying definitions and nuances of competency, the remainder of this chapter will focus on the more general medical, psychiatric, and functional (behavioral) assessments that can be made of persons whose functional abilities, including judgment and decision making, are in question before the court. The three types of assessment describe what can be done, but not necessarily what is done, in making an evaluation of medical, psychiatric, and functional conditions in guardianship cases. The assessments described here are not ordinarily done in guardianship cases, perhaps because the respondent's functional capacity is clearly deteriorated or, more probably, because of the cost of making the assessments.

Medical Assessments

Medical illness and subclinical disease states can produce changes in cognitive functions such as judgment and in behavior in the older person. The older person with diabetes who misses a meal or misreads the numbers on the syringe experiences a fluctuation in glucose levels that produces a transient change in the person's cognitive functioning. In another case, the older person with breast disease metastatic to the brain has a fixed deficit in cognitive function that may be further exacerbated by a superimposed delirium. Although the delirium will resolve with the treatment of the underlying precipitant, the baseline cognitive functioning of this patient has been altered permanently due to the malignant process.

In order to determine the extent to which the observed cognitive functioning and judgment of the person have been affected by the presence of an existing or new medical illness, a thorough assessment of the individual's medical history is required. Beginning with a review of systems, current symptoms, if any, for each system can be identified. The presence of shortness of breath, fatigue, and edema of the lower extremities suggests impairment in the cardiovascular system that may be confirmed with a history of exertional dyspnea. Urinary urgency and frequency with a recent history of discomfort or burning on urination suggest the presence of a urinary tract infection. The medical history should continue to determine past medical problems and prior surgical procedures. It may be necessary to remind the older person to report medical illnesses and surgical procedures that occurred in their youth. The current medications of the older person require careful review. These include medications that are prescribed, saved, and borrowed from friends and neighbors. Financial means are a concern for the majority of elders regardless of actual financial circumstances. As medications are one of the costliest items in their budget, older persons attempt to minimize costs by "stretching" medications purchased and by sharing with other older friends with similar symptoms medications that have alleviated specific symptoms. Over-the-counter medications should be explored. The antihistamine effects of a cold medicine combined with a tricyclic antidepressant can result in a pattern of daytime somnolence and episodic disorientation and confusion.

A physical examination needs to be conducted. The presence of bruises, partly healed scars, skin abrasions or marks suggesting the use of restraints requires further exploration. The older person may need encouragement to talk about neglect or abuse by a care giver, particularly if the older person is dependent on this person for care. Evidence of neglect may appear in unkempt clothing, signs of infrequent bathing, and poor skin care, with the presence of skin breakdown or ulcers. The lack of stability in a chronic medical problem such as diabetes or hypertension that had been well managed before the onset of frailty in the older person necessitated the assistance of a care giver may also suggest neglect.

Laboratory studies can be completed based on the working differential diagnosis determined from the history, physical examination, information from the family and/or care giver, and the patient's medical record. If a recent change in level of arousal or cognitive functioning has been noted, skull films and a computed tomography (CT) scan of the head may be indicated. If a recent cerebrovascular accident or stroke is suspected, a neurological consultation may be advisable.

The medical assessment of the older patient for whom the issue of competency has been raised requires that the person receive a thorough evaluation for the changes in cognitive function. Drug-drug interactions, new onset diabetes or stroke, an episode of delirium caused by a variety of factors, and depression are the more frequent causes of altered cognitive function. The older person with altered cognitive function who has not experienced these changes should be evaluated further for less frequent causes. The presence of neglect or abuse of the older person must also be considered. A tentative or frankly fearful response to a care giver or a silent, withdrawn, nonresponsive older person described by friends as previously being outgoing warrants careful evaluation by the health care team. The identification of an at-risk situation with mental illness or substance abuse in a care giver who clearly appears stressed requires immediate intervention. An assessment of the family situation by a social worker can provide important data to facilitate the most efficacious intervention for the benefit of the psychologically, financially, or physically abused elder.

Psychiatric Assessments

The request for a psychiatric consultation to assess the competence of an older person can result from any of the legal areas, such as refusal to consent to life-saving medical treatment or guardianship. Depending on the specific legal competency at issue, the psychiatrist will include a specific series of questions related to that matter.

The psychiatric assessment begins with a history of the current problem or situation as understood by the person. The person is asked to detail past medical history and use of current medications (prescribed, borrowed, and over-the-counter medications). Then, the social network of the person is explored. "Do you live with someone? Where do you live? Describe the setting for me. Are members of your family alive? Where do they live? How often do you see them? Do you have a church that you attend regularly? Do church members call or visit you? Are you a member of a social club or union or fraternal organization? How often do you get together with other members? How many people visit you in a week? How many people call you in a week? Are people likely to drop by to visit you? How often does this happen?"

The person is encouraged to describe how the current problem or situation has affected his or her functioning. What changes have occurred in daily functioning? If there are limitations in physical abilities such as difficulty climbing stairs or confinement to a wheelchair, how does the person feel about these changes? Is the person able to articulate his or her feelings about the changes in daily routine? Are there changes in sleep patterns, in appetite and weight, and in the level of sexual feelings? Does the person have problems with constipation? Is it more difficult to concentrate? Does the person experience a sense of sadness and find that he or she is near tears or cries frequently when thinking about how life has changed?

To the extent they are available, the person's medical records are reviewed. Current laboratory data and medications are reviewed to determine the physiologic state of the patient as well as the potential for drug-drug interactions (Baker, et al., 1986; Baker & Finkel, 1988; Sadoff, 1991) affecting the level of arousal and the cognitive function of the individual. With these data on the biologic, psychologic, and social status of the patient, the formal mental status examination is begun.

Formal assessment of orientation is initiated. "What is today's date, in other words, the month, date, year, and day of the week. Where are we now? What is the name of this building? Can you tell me your full name? How old are you, today?" Based on the initial part of the psychiatric assessment in which the person's educational level, work history, and religious orientation were obtained, the psychiatric consultant has information that determines the specific manner in which questions are presented. The words and syntax used with a retired college president will be different from those used with an individual who completed only 5 years of formal education. If during the course of the interview, however, it becomes apparent that the retired college president has significant deficits in word finding, difficulty in sustaining attention, and limited recall of new information, then the words used by the psychiatrist and the complexity of syntax may differ little between these two persons, which in itself provides additional information about the current cognitive functioning of the retired professor who earned a doctoral degree.

Attention, registration of new information, and recall of that information can be assessed quite quickly. Does the person remember your name from your introduction? If not, can the person recall it after you reintroduce yourself? Can the person repeat seven digits forward (a telephone number) and four or more digits backwards? Can the person recall three of three objects 5 minutes after being told the objects? Can the person state the year of marriage, high school graduation, or first fulltime employment?

The assessment of the various components of memory are an important part of the mental status examination. Does the person recall his or her mother's name? Can the person state the maiden name of his or her mother? Did the person describe in the history events that occurred during the last year and the past 5 years without difficulty? Does the medical chart confirm the information the person gave about medical illnesses, hospitalizations, death of siblings or spouse, and moves? Can the person tell what was eaten at the last meal? Can the person describe what he or she did in the preceding 24 hours? These questions access remote, long-term, intermediate, and recent memory. The digit span test and recall of the interviewer's name assess immediate memory, as does the recall of three objects.

Cognitive capacity includes the ability of the person to manipulate information and to use the information in the solution of a problem. Serial sevens assess problem solving with mathematics. "Can you subtract 7 from 100? Now, subtract 7 from each new number all the way down." If the educational attainment is less than sixth grade, the person is asked to subtract 3 from 20 and to continue the serial substraction of 3 from the result.

Language function was addressed during the history-taking process. Did the person understand your questions? Was it necessary to simplify your vocabulary? Was it necessary to change from compound sentences to simple sentences in order for the person to understand your questions? The naming of objects should be asked as part of the mental status examination. A silent cerebrovascular accident (CVA) may have been undetected by the person and the person's family and friends. Difficulty with naming and articulation ("Repeat this phrase for me—no ifs, ands, or buts"—on formal cognitive testing) may provide the first clue that an undiagnosed CVA has occurred.

The presence of abnormal thought processes are then assessed. Have you had difficulty concentrating recently? Are your thoughts speeded up or racing? Are you able to stop or to interrupt the racing thoughts? Have you heard voices that others do not hear? Are these voices commenting about you? Are the voices threatening you? Are the voices telling you what to do? Do you believe that someone is controlling your thoughts? Have you seen things that other people did not see? How did you feel about these things? Do you believe that someone is trying to harm you? Who is trying to harm you? Why are they trying to harm you?

The mental status examination explores changes in mood. A manic person has difficulty concentrating and is speeded up so that the ability to attend and to process information effectively in order to make a decision is impaired. The depressed person experiences slowed thinking and is indecisive. Decision making is impaired in this case due to ambivalence and indecisiveness. "How would you describe your mood? Have you felt okay, happy, very happy, or the happiest that you've ever been in life? Have your family and friends noted the change in your mood? Do you feel sad, blue, or down? How do you feel about the future? Do you feel hopeless and/or helpless about being able to change things that are worrying you? Have you had thoughts about wanting to go to sleep and not wake up (passive suicidal ideation)? Have you had thoughts about wanting to end your life . . . to kill yourself? Have you tried to end your life (suicide attempt)? Did you tell anyone about your attempt to end your life?" Older persons constitute about 13% of the U.S. population but complete about 25% of the suicides in the U.S. Thus, the presence of suicidal ideation and the presence of a suicidal plan must be assessed in older persons in most areas of legal competency.

With these baseline data, the consulting psychiatrist then addresses with the person the specific legal area generating the request for competency assessment and explores the person's rationale for his or her decisions.

Functional Assessments

The functional assessments described in this section do not focus on the functional abilities described earlier in this chapter. Those functional abilities described earlier are cognitive or intellectual abilities such as ability to understand information, to compare pros and cons, and to make decisions.

The functional activities of concern here are the physical activities carried out by the elderly person that are commonly termed "activities of daily living" (ADL) and "instrumental activities of daily living" (IADL). ADL comprise activities needed to take care of bodily needs and ordinarily consist of bathing, dressing, clothing, toileting, and feeding oneself. IADL comprise more complicated activities needed to maintain a household and include activities such as shopping, doing housework, preparing meals, taking medicine, and using the telephone.

There is a clear distinction between cognitive abilities and ADL. An older person may know that he should take his medicine and makes the decision to do so, but if he cannot unscrew the cap off the bottle of medicine he cannot take his medicine by himself.

The issue of ADL arises because persons in their 70s and older do not have the physical strength, endurance, and mobility that they had when younger, even when they were in their 50s and 60s. Thus, older persons may experience increasing physical frailty on the basis of ordinary age-related changes or superimposed chronic medical problems, or both. Older persons may then have diminished physical abilities as they strive to meet the ordinary and occasional extraordinary demands of everyday life.

If persons require no assistance or only minimal assistance with ADL, they can usually live independently. If the person has difficulty walking more than one block from home, is unable to use the telephone because of vision or hearing problems, or is unable to shop for groceries, the older person still may be able to live alone. Although impaired in IADL, a home health aide or a schedule of family and friends can assist the older person with shopping. New technology may enable the hearing-impaired elder to use the telephone. If legally blind, the elder's sense of touch can be used to either dial a number using raised large numbers on the phone dial or to identify the location of the operator button to obtain phone numbers through operator assistance.

In a guardianship case, the court is interested in the extent to which the physical abilities of the older person affect the person's ability to care for himself or herself. Specific illustrations of competence in obtaining basic supplies (food and clothing), maintaining a safe and clean living environment, and being able to obtain emergency help are important data for the judicial process of guardianship. Specific illustrations of how the older person has or has not maintained their residence and their personal hygiene will aid the judge in determining the person's competence to manage basic needs. In addition, there are a variety of instruments that have been developed solely or in part to provide measures of ADL and IADL (Grisso, 1986; Kane & Kane, 1981).

SUMMARY

The major determination that must be made by the court in guardianship cases concerns the competence of the respondent. Does the person have the decision-making capacity to make the decisions required to care for self and for financial assets? Decision making requires various functional abilities and carrying out decisions requires additional but different functions or activities. Unfortunately for the court, there is no one standard proven method of assessing competency. This chapter contains a description of three general forms of assessment of respondents that can provide information of use to the court in adjudicating competency, however.

REFERENCES

Applebaum, P. S., & Grisso, T. (1988). Assessing patients' capabilities to consent to treatment. *New England Journal of Medicine, 319*(25), 1635–1638.

Baker, F. M., & Finkel, S. I. (1988). Legal issues in geriatric psychiatry. In L.W. Lazarus (Ed.), *Essentials in geriatric psychiatry* (pp. 214–229). New York: Springer.

Baker, F. M., Perr, I. N., & Yesavage, J. A. (1986). *An overview of legal issues in geriatric psychiatry.* Washington, DC: American Psychiatric Association.

Fitten, L. J., Lusky, R., & Hamann, C. (1990). Assessing treatment decision-making capacity in elderly nursing home residents. *Journal of the American Geriatric Society, 38*(10), 1097–1104.

Grisso, T. (1986). *Evaluating competencies: Forensic assessments and instruments.* New York: Plenum.

Haddad, A. M. (1988). Determining competency. *Journal of Gerontological Nursing, 14*(6), 19–22.

High, D. M. (1994). Surrogate decision-making: Who will make decisions for me when I can't? *Clinics in Geriatric Medicine, 10*(3), 445–461.

Kane, R., & Kane, R. (1981). *Assessing the Elderly: A practical guide to measurement.* Lexington, MA: Lexington.

Kapp, M. B. (1990). Evaluating decision making capacity in the elderly: A review of recent literature. *Journal of Elder Abuse and Neglect, 2*(3/4), 15–29.

Kapp, M. B. & Mossman, D. (1996). Measuring decisional capacity: Cautions on the construction of a "Capacimeter." *Psychology, Public Policy, and Law, 2*(1), 73–95.

Lang, D. J. (1980). Geriatric, psychiatric, and legal aspects of the mental state of the aged. *Legal Medicine Quarterly*, 4, 161–174.

Lo, B. (1990). Assessing decision-making capacity. *Law, Medicine & Health Care, 18*(3), 193–201.

Sadoff, R. L. (1991). Medical-legal issues. In J. Sadavoy, L. W. Lazarus, & L. F. Jarvik (Eds.), *Comprehensive review of geriatric psychiatry* (pp. 637–651). Washington, DC: American Psychiatric Press.

Weisensee, M. G., & Kjervik, D. K. (1989). Dilemmas in decision making for caregivers of cognitively impaired elderly persons. *Journal of Professional Nursing, 5*(4), 186–191.

CHAPTER 4

Psychiatric Disorders Affecting Competency

Donald P. Hay, Linda K. Hay, and Gwen E. Fagala

C apacity to receive and evaluate information and to make and communicate decisions can be affected by mental disorders. Broad categories of mental or psychiatric disorders are classified specifically in the Diagnostic and Statistical Manual of Mental Disorders, Fourth Edition (DSM IV), published by the American Psychiatric Association (APA) (1994). These categories include disorders such as delirium, dementia, and amnestic and other cognitive disorders; mental disorders due to a general medical condition not elsewhere classified; substance-related disorders; schizophrenia and other psychotic disorders; mood disorders; anxiety disorders; somatoform disorders; factitious disorders; dissociative disorders; sexual and gender identity disorders; eating disorders; sleep disorders; impulse-control disorders; adjustment disorders; and personality disorders.

Obviously, a chapter summarizing the varying effects of these disorders on the ability of an elderly individual to process information and make decisions would be difficult to execute and to absorb. In the interest of relevance and clarity, this chapter addresses the three most predominant psychiatric disorders seen in the elderly. Mood disorders, cognitive disorders, and psychotic disorders are described with respect to their clinical aspects, their effect on decision making, and their reversibility and prognosis.

For the best possible assessment and diagnosis of competency related to mental disorders such as mood disorders, cognitive disorders, or psychotic disorders, the psychiatrist and, when available, the geriatric psychiatrist are best suited to make these determinations.

MOOD DISORDERS

The classification "mood disorders" refers to depressive disorders such as major depression and dysthymia and to bipolar disorders commonly known as "manic depression." Mood disorders, especially depression, frequently involve both situational aspects or external precipitating events such as the death of a loved one or the loss of a job as well as biologic factors such as neurochemical imbalances linked to hereditary factors and other medical occurrences.

Major Depressive Disorder

The prevalence of *major depressive disorder* in the elderly has been reported as 1% to 2% in the community-dwelling population, approaching 5% in primary care settings, and 15% to 20% in nursing homes (National Institutes of Health [NIH] Consensus Conference, 1992; Zubenko, et al., 1994). The *symptoms of depression* may occur in as much as 15% of the community-dwelling older adult population (NIH Consensus Conference, 1992; Zubenko, et al., 1994).

Depression is perhaps one of the most critical and yet easily overlooked issues in evaluating and treating the elderly individual. Elderly persons may be reluctant to seek psychiatric treatment, they may attribute emotional symptoms to physical causes, and they may have complications from multiple chronic systemic diseases. In addition, many elderly individuals are fearful of exhibiting signs and symptoms of "senility" and the implication of chronic mental decline. The initial experience of mood changes and the cognitive changes such as forgetfulness or difficulty concentrating that may accompany depressed mood may lead an elderly individual to avoid medical evaluation for fear of being diagnosed with dementia.

Evaluation must begin with a search for possible medical causes for depression. Many medical conditions such as hypothyroidism, Parkinson's disease, and strokes directly cause depressive symptoms. In addition, the medications used to treat systemic diseases such as certain antihypertensives or eye drops for glaucoma can cause symptoms of depression.

Once medical causes of depression are ruled out or treated, the evaluation of an elderly person for depression proceeds psychiatrically, ordinarily by using the nine symptoms of major depressive disorder described in the DSM IV (APA, 1994, pp. 320–323). As summarized in the acronymic mnemonic CEASE SAAD©, the symptoms (see Table 4.1) include concentration difficulties; decrease in energy; increase in anxiety or agitation; spontaneous crying or depressed mood; sleeping difficulties; suicidal ideation or thoughts of harming oneself; anhedonia or difficulty in experiencing pleasure in usual activities; appetite disturbances often accompanied by weight loss or gain; and excessive worrying, feelings of helplessness, or overwhelming feelings of guilt. Also available are a variety of scales such as the Geriatric Depression Scale (Yesavage, et al., 1983) and the Zung Depression Scale (Zung, 1965). Major depressive disorder in its more severe forms may be accompanied by psychotic thoughts or delusions, including

TABLE 4.1 CEASE SAAD©

Using the Scale

C	Concentration difficulties (8)*
E	Energy low (6)*
A	Anxiety high (5)*
S	Spontaneous crying (1)*
E	Early morning awakening (4)*
S	Suicidal (9)*
A	Appetite disturbed (3)*
A	Anhedonia (2)*
D	Derogatory feelings and guilt feelings (7)*

*Number in parentheses corresponds to the DSM-IV (APA, 1994, pp. 320–323).
Each of the above categories must be assessed by questioning patients as to their subjective awareness of these symptoms or as reported by family members or friends when the patients are unable to answer the questions. If the patients are unable to verbalize their symptoms, it is helpful to supply them with choices for their answers. An example for "Concentration" is to ask patients if they can read the newspaper or watch their favorite television show.

the hearing of voices, feelings of paranoia, and delusional thoughts not unlike schizophrenia.

Once the diagnosis is made, treating major depressive disorder can be accomplished by providing a combination of psychotherapeutic and biologic interventions. Psychotherapy may be supportive or psychodynamic depending on the level of function and ability of the individual. Most psychotherapy is aimed at helping the individual become aware of the role that psychological factors play in his or her depression such as relationship problems, passivity versus assertiveness, and how he or she communicates feelings to others.

Biologic intervention may be provided by psychopharmacologic means, such as the use of an antidepressant medication. There are many groups of antidepressants available, and clinicians usually prescribe a particular type and dose based on potential side effects for the individual and his or her specific symptoms. The antidepressants that may cause sedation as a side effect may be used for individuals with depression who are having difficulty sleeping and therefore may be given at bedtime. The antidepressants that may promote activity as a side effect may be used for individuals with depression who are having difficulty getting up, and they are, therefore, given in the morning. Other side effects to be considered include anticholinergic effects (dry mouth, urinary retention, constipation, or confusion), effects on cardiac function, and gastrointestinal irritation.

In general, antidepressant medications are designed to enhance certain neurochemicals that are believed to be relatively deficient in depressed individuals. Thus, the goal of medication treatment is to restore a proper neurochemical balance and thus reduce symptoms. In the past, antidepressant medication was initiated until symptoms subsided and often discontinued and only resumed if symptoms returned, which could be months or years later. Controlled studies have shown however, that those individuals who have had three or more episodes of major depression do best with lifetime treatment (Kupfer, et al., 1992) with relatively benign antidepressants with low side effect profiles and that this is preferable to allowing a possible relapse or recurrence of symptoms, which in more severe cases may lead to hospitalization and many days away from work and family. Most individuals with chronic depressive disorders respond well to a combination of medication and psychotherapy and are able to live normal lives with almost complete absence of symptoms.

If an individual does not respond to the usual medications for depression, electroconvulsive therapy (ECT) may be initiated. ECT, through electrical initiation of seizures, results in the enhancement of neurochemicals such as occurs with the use of antidepressant medications. Formerly known as "shock treatment," this much misunderstood, feared, and maligned treatment modality continues to be recognized by many psychiatrists as an extremely effective and safe treatment for late-life depression, with positive response rates of 70% to 80% (APA, 1990; Mulsant, Rosen, Thorton, & Zubenko, 1991; NIH Consensus Conference, 1992; Zubenko, et al., 1994). ECT has also been shown to be relatively safe and effective in the medically ill elderly (Hay, 1989). ECT has been refined since its inception almost 60 years ago, so that the patient usually does not experience any discomfort and few, if any, side effects. Unfortunately, the general population is not aware of the advances in its use, and often this treatment modality is reserved only as a last effort to reverse the symptoms of severe refractory depression.

Effects on Competency

Many aspects of mood disorders can affect the competency of an individual. The symptoms of depression, believed to be caused by decreased neurochemicals, in essence represent an impairment of brain function. A typical profile of a depressed individual may include difficulties with concentration, remembering details, and easy distractibility. Decreased concentration, for example, may lead to difficulty with memory and an inability to make decisions. In addition, low energy, anxiety, depressed mood, suicidal thoughts, helplessness, and, in severe forms, psychotic thoughts most definitely change the way an individual processes information and makes decisions about his or her life.

A complicating aspect of impaired decision making resulting from depression is an unusual paradox. The very organ (the brain) that is affected by the illness (major depression) is the same entity (the mind) that needs to make a decision, for example, about whether or not to accept treatment as a patient with a serious or life-threatening medical illness. One of the more overwhelming aspects of major depression is the creation of the feelings of inadequacy, low self-esteem and low self-worth. Such self-deprecatory feelings frequently lead to the individual requesting to stop all further treatment as a result of feeling that he or she is not worthy of the efforts being made to help.

It is difficult to evaluate the effect of depression on a patient's capacity to make medical decisions, however. The depression may be seen as a reasonable response to serious medical illness, the depressed patient has fewer obvious or less overt changes in decision-making ability than a psychotic or delirious patient has, and a diagnosis of depression is neither necessary nor sufficient to determine that the patient's ability to make medical decisions is impaired. The task of differentiating those situations in which depression impairs the capacity to make medical decisions from those in which it does not is best accomplished by a systematic approach for the assessment of competence including a thorough medical and psychiatric evaluation (see chapter 3).

With proper evaluation and treatment, depression is reversible so that an individual's decision-making capacity may be restored to previous levels. A small subgroup of depressed individuals may remain treatment resistant and must undergo more aggressive treatment measures such as multiple medications and ongoing ECT. In general, however, if an individual has been properly diagnosed and treated with the appropriate dose of antidepressant medication, he or she is able to function normally.

Dysthymia

The symptoms of dysthymia are similar to those of major depression, but dysthymia is a more chronic form of depression of at least 2 years' duration. Treatment of dysthymia may be best accomplished with psychotherapy, medication, or both. Competency may be affected at the more severe stages of the illness.

As defined by DSM IV (APA, 1994, pp. 345–349), dysthymia is a chronic form of depression lasting at least 2 years. Approximately 6% of the population suffer from dysthymia sometime during their lifetime. Symptoms of dysthymia include depressed mood, increased or decreased appetite, insomnia or hypersomnia, decreased energy, poor self-esteem, poor concentration, and feelings of hopelessness. These symptoms are similar to those of major depression but not as severe, and suicidal thoughts or psychotic symptoms are not present in dysthymia. People with dysthymia may have episodes of major depression superimposed on their chronic symptoms. This is sometimes called "double depression." Dysthymia may be treated with psychotherapy or antidepressant medication.

Bipolar Disorder

In the DSM IV (APA, 1994, pp. 350–363) bipolar disorder, or "manic depression," is characterized by periods of depression alternating with periods of mania or hyperactivity and agitation. Bipolar disorder affects approximately 1% of the population. The symptoms of the depressed phase of bipolar disorder are identical to those of major depression, discussed previously. Manic phases are characterized by symptoms of elevated, irritable, or expansive mood, inflated self-esteem, grandiose ideas, decreased need for sleep, increased activity, talkativeness, racing thoughts, distractibility, and poor judgment. Persons in a manic state may engage in activities that, while pleasurable, may cause adverse consequences, such as spending money foolishly, engaging in sexual indiscretions, or behaving in a reckless manner. Severe manic episodes may include psychotic symptoms, such as hallucinations or delusions. Mixed episodes, in which the person has symptoms of both mania and depression simultaneously, may also occur.

Bipolar disorder is a chronic illness characterized by periods of illness interspersed with periods of normal mood. Although there is no cure, the symptoms of bipolar disorder can be controlled with medications. Lithium and anticonvulsant medications, as well as antidepressants when needed, are used to treat acute episodes of bipolar disorder and to prevent recurrences. Bipolar disorder may also be treated with ECT. With proper treatment, people with bipolar disorder can often function normally.

COGNITIVE DISORDERS

Cognitive functioning consists of a variety of processes including decision making, judgment, long- and short-term memory, reasoning, calculation, learning, and problem solving. Since decision making is a cognitive process, cognitive disorders are particularly relevant to the courts' task of adjudicating competence.

Impairment in cognitive function can result from many known disorders. These disorders include primary brain disease such as psychiatric illnesses, brain tumors, and strokes and diseases of other organ systems such as hypothyroidism or diabetes that result in secondary brain disease. Impairment in cognitive function can also result from any medication or side effect of medications used to treat medical illnesses. Finally, cognitive impairments resulting from these disorders may be reversible, be constant, or become progressively worse.

Reversibility is an important consideration in the courts' deliberations about incompetency. If a respondent's current state of decision-making incapacity can be reversed to capacity by effectively treating the disease or condition producing the incapacity, then the court may postpone the case until the treatment is completed and another evaluation is made of the respondent.

Delirium

Delirium is an impairment in cognitive functioning occurring as a temporary, reversible phenomenon and may be related to medication side effects or the reversible effects of a metabolic illness. There are as many as 80 possible causes of delirium, and a complete medical evaluation is necessary to investigate etiology and treatment (Conn, 1991). The hallmark of delirium is an impairment of the ability to focus, maintain, and shift attention. The individual experiencing delirium may have symptoms of cognitive impairment that fluctuate during the day.

Dementia

Geriatric psychiatrists are often consulted to determine whether a patient is experiencing delirium, which when identified is treated medically. When delirium has been ruled out as a cause of cognitive impairment, the focus of investigation becomes that of dementia. Dementia has been defined as an acquired syndrome of intellectual impairment produced by brain dysfunction (Cummings & Benson, 1992). The essential factors to be aware of when considering a diagnosis of dementia include the previous level of functioning of the individual and the duration of the symptoms in terms of weeks and months as opposed to days and hours, which would more likely indicate delirium. According to the DSM IV (APA, 1994, pp. 133–155), dementia is divided into several categories, including dementia of the Alzheimer's type, vascular dementia, dementia due to other medical conditions, substance-induced persisting dementia, and dementia due to multiple etiologies. Amnestic disorders involving partial or total loss of memory due to medical conditions and substance abuse are classified separately from dementia in the DSM IV, as are other cognitive disorders, including impairment in cognition due to medical conditions or postconcussional disorders.

Prevalence of Dementia

Since most dementias are found in individuals over 65, and that population is increasing at a rapid rate, it could be said that dementia is approaching epidemic proportions. The prevalence of dementia as reported in the literature is extremely variable, 2.5% to 24.6% in those over 65 (Ineichen, 1987), due to the variability of the types and ages of populations studied. The prevalence of different types of dementia is also difficult to ascertain because the studies of prevalence tend to have an overrepresentation of hospital based patient populations that, in general, have more severe intellectual deficits resulting from progressive disorders such as Alzheimer's or vascular dementias. It could be said, however, that the most common type of dementia is the Alzheimer's type (50%), and the second most common type is vascular dementia (20%), with a combination of the two (15%–20%) being the third most common (Cummings & Benson, 1992).

Cortical versus Subcortical Dementias

An important classification of dementia is by location of the area of the brain primarily affected based on patterns of neuropsychological deficits. These classifications are helpful in understanding etiology and in formulating a diagnosis.

Cortical dementias result when the cerebral cortex or the outer parts of the brain are affected, for example, by Alzheimer's disease or Pick's disease. Subcortical dementias result when internal brain structures are affected by diseases such as Huntington's disease, Parkinson's disease, Wilson's disease, and others. These are diseases that produce maximal dysfunction in the areas of the brain involving impairment of movement as well as cognition.

The cortical types of dementia produce disruption of functional abilities important in competency. These disruptions include naming difficulties, impaired comprehension, memory disturbances, calculating difficulty, and poor judgment. In general, personality remains intact and the basic neurological examination remains normal until the late stages of these diseases. Frontotemporal dementia is an even more specific classification or syndrome of cortical dementias that involves the frontal and temporal lobes predominantly (Kumar & Gottlieb, 1993).

The subcortical dementias likewise produce disruption of cognitive processes. In contrast to the disruptions due to cortical dementias, those due to subcortical dementias include slowing of cognition, speech, and comprehension. There is also difficulty in retrieving information and, in the noncognitive realm, changes in mood. The individual suffering from a cortical dementia may not be able to remember three objects after 5 minutes due to the inability to process new information, but the individual with a subcortical dementia may be able to retrieve these from memory, albeit very slowly and with reminders.

Diagnostic Issues

The initial consideration in diagnosing dementia is that all medical causes have been considered and ruled out by a thorough medical workup. Following this, the mental status of the individual is determined by taking a history and conducting a formal mental assessment. Screening tests are helpful initially to determine severity and to characterize the dementia. A widely used test, The Folstein Mini Mental Status Exam (Folstein, Folstein, & McHugh, 1975), is a short series of problems that assess a variety of mental functions, including short-term memory, calculations, orientation, spacial orientation, and the ability to follow directions.

A longer examination is indicated in most situations. The clinician considers the appropriate aspects of the cognitive deficit in each particular patient based on his or her particular needs as well as daily living activities (Nishimura & Kobayashi, 1993). Among the areas to assess are the state of awareness; general appearance and behavior; mood and affect; speech and language; motor aspects of speech; language functions; visuospatial functions; additional cortical functions such as purposeful movements, ability to navigate in familiar areas, and right-left orientation; and cognitive functions such as memory, calculation, thought content, and patient–examiner relationship.

Alzheimer's Disease

Alois Alzheimer in 1907 first described the disease that represents the most frequently diagnosed dementia. It has been estimated that there were 1,414,000 cases of Alzheimer's in the United States in 1980 and that there will be 2,008,000 in the year 2000. The incidence and prevalence of Alzheimer's (Dementia of Alzheimer's Type [DAT]) is positively correlated with age. The terms presenile and senile dementia, formerly used to differentiate age of onset before 65 and after, is no longer applicable since it has been found that both age groups experience similar pathology irrespective of age of onset. There is evidence of familial inheritance comprising 20% of reported cases of DAT, and some studies suggest that this group is more likely to have a more rapidly progressing illness.

Diagnosis of DAT is only determined upon autopsy with microscopic study of the brain cells. Probable DAT is diagnosed clinically prior to death, however, with high accuracy based on having ruled out any other possible causes of dementia and careful consideration of the global clinical picture and the history of the patient. The most significant characteristic of DAT is a steadily progressive decline in cognition, usually divided into three stages based on severity of symptoms (Reisberg, et al., 1987). The progression of stages is variable in length, with Stage I ranging from 1 to 3 years, Stage II from 2 to 10 years, and Stage III from 8 to 12 years.

The initial stage is usually experienced as memory disturbance but also includes poor judgment, carelessness, indifference, irritability, and suspiciousness. The second stage contains aphasia or difficulty with language and apraxia or difficulty in carrying out purposeful activities upon command, in addition to the worsening of other deficits. Pacing, restlessness, and occasional incontinence occurs. In the last stage there is severe impairment of all intellectual functioning, with physical impairment and both urinary and fecal incontinence.

The etiology of DAT is unknown. Aluminum toxicity, immune dysfunction, viral infection, cellular filament deficits such as "neurofibrillary tangles" and "amyloid plaques," and hereditary factors have all been considered as possible causes.

There is no treatment for DAT at this time, but many strategies have been developed to treat the symptoms. Various agents that promote increases in certain brain chemicals found to be decreased in Alzheimer's patients are being investigated for use in improving impaired cognitive and memory functions. One agent that is currently available by prescription (tacrine) has been found to be somewhat effective in improving cognition in selected patients with DAT. Other symptomatic treatment includes medications for management of the behavioral manifestations of the decreased cognition such as agitation, antidepressant medications for the frequently occurring depressive symptoms in DAT, and antipsychotic medications for the more severely unmanageable patients.

The course of DAT usually requires significant support and social services for the patient and family. Once diagnosed, a variety of family decisions need to be addressed as patients slowly lose their ability to comprehend their own situation and to care for themselves. The *36-Hour Day* (Mace & Rabins, 1991) is a useful book for the family of the affected individual.

Pick's Disease

Arnold Pick described this progressive dementia in 1892. It includes similar symptoms to those of DAT but is characterized as involving more personality changes in the initial stages, including apathy, irritability, depression, jocularity, and euphoria, with socially inappropriate behavior. As with DAT, there are no definitive diagnostic criteria in terms of laboratory studies although such studies are necessary to rule out other causes of dementia. Upon autopsy, definite "Pick's bodies" or dense intracellular structures can be seen microscopically in brain cells. As with DAT, there is no known etiology for Pick's disease and treatment is symptomatic.

Vascular Dementias

In the past the term "hardening of the arteries" was frequently used to describe senility. The hardening of arteries was thought to result in poor circulation in the brain, which caused the progressive cognitive problems. This idea has been abandoned because little correlation was found between vascular involvement and the extent and severity of brain pathology found in dementia patients. Currently, it has been shown that multiple cerebral infarctions, or mini-strokes, can result in dementia and that these vascular dementias can be recognized clinically. Actually the term vascular dementia is all encompassing and includes a variety of syndromes following hemorrhagic events, including single strokes. Multi-infarct dementia (MID), one type of vascular dementia, refers to multiple cerebrovascular occlusions whereby brain tissue destruction occurs, accounting for the cognitive decline.

In general, vascular dementias differ from DAT in that they have an earlier age of onset; affect men more than women; have a more abrupt onset, a stepwise deterioration, and a fluctuating course; and are associated with a history of hypertension. The most important difference affecting the course of vascular dementias, as opposed to DAT, is that the progression of cognitive loss may be halted with proper management of associated medical conditions such as hypertension, whereas in DAT the progression is inevitable.

Implications for Competency

In summary, the concept of cognitive disorders is divided into temporary and permanent or progressive disorders. Delirium is related to a temporary situation such as systemic illness and in most cases can be resolved and the cognitive incapacity reversed. Dementias are usually progressive and irreversible and are produced by a variety of forms of brain dysfunction. Thus, it is essential, when evaluating an individual for competency, that the first step be a thorough assessment to rule out any temporary causes of cognitive dysfunction. If temporary causes are not found, then it is necessary to differentiate between the types of dementia that are progressive and the types such as vascular dementias that, although irreversible, may be controlled so that the cognitive impairment does not progress further. Once a relatively accurate diagnosis has been achieved by a thorough physical and mental status examination and laboratory tests, a clinician such as a psychiatrist (or when available a geriatric psychiatrist) can reasonably predict the average course of the dementias and how this course is likely to affect the cognitive abilities of the individual.

PSYCHOTIC DISORDERS

Psychotic disorders are characterized by symptoms such as hallucinations, delusions, disorganized thinking, and bizarre behavior. Hallucinations are false sensory perceptions not triggered by real sensory stimuli. They may involve any sensory modality—vision, hearing, touch, taste, or smell. Delusions are fixed false beliefs, tenaciously held despite evidence to the contrary. Some psychotic disorders that may occur in the elderly are schizophrenia, delusional disorder, psychotic disorders due to general medical conditions, substance-induced psychotic disorders, and mood disorders with psychotic features. Following a description of types of psychotic disorders, their implications for competency will be discussed.

Schizophrenia

Schizophrenia is a serious psychotic disorder affecting approximately 1% of the general population. Schizophrenia most commonly develops in early adulthood and generally continues throughout life. It has been estimated, however, that 13% of hospitalized schizophrenic patients have onset of their disease in their 50s, 7% in their 60s, and 3% after age 70 (Harris & Jeste, 1988). The symptoms of schizophrenia are frequently categorized as either positive or negative. The positive symptoms include hallucinations, delusions, disorganized thinking, and bizarre behavior. The negative symptoms include blunted emotional responses, social isolation, and lack of motivation. Schizophrenia can also be divided into various subtypes according to which symptoms are most prominent in a given individual. The subtypes of schizophrenia included in DSM IV (APA, 1994, pp. 286–290) are paranoid, disorganized, catatonic, undifferentiated, and residual schizophrenia.

Schizophrenia is usually a chronic disease, although some individuals may have symptom-free periods followed by relapses, and some may even recover completely. Persons with schizophrenia are at high risk for suicide and also have a higher than usual mortality rate from medical illnesses and trauma. Although there is no known cure for schizophrenia, many of the symptoms can be relieved with antipsychotic medication. The positive symptoms, such as hearing of voices, tend to respond to treatment better than the negative symptoms, such as lack of close interpersonal relationships.

Psychosocial treatments are also often helpful in aiding patients to deal with the consequences of their illness and to learn to function as well as possible in society.

Delusional Disorder

Delusional disorder is characterized by the presence of one or more nonbizarre (that is, they could actually happen in real life) delusions for a period of at least one month. Hallucinations, disorganized thinking, and bizarre behavior are not present, although the person's behavior may be influenced by the delusions. The DSM IV (APA, 1994, pp. 296–298) divides delusional disorder into subtypes based on the predominant theme of the delusions. In the erotomanic type, the person believes that someone, often famous or of higher status, is in love with him or her. The grandiose type is characterized by delusions of inflated worth, power, knowledge, fame, or a special relationship with God or a celebrity. In the jealous type, the person believes that his or her sexual partner is unfaithful. Individuals with the persecutory type believe that they are being persecuted in some way.

The somatic type is characterized by the belief that one has a physical disease or defect. There are also mixed and unspecified types.

Delusional disorder affects approximately 0.03% of the population and usually has its onset after the age of 40 years. Some studies have suggested that sensory deficits, such as hearing impairment, are associated with the development of delusional disorders (Cooper & Curry, 1976). Delusional disorder tends to be chronic, although some individuals may have waxing and waning of their symptoms. Antipsychotic medications may be effective in treating delusional disorder. Delusional disorder in the elderly is frequently treated most effectively with ECT (Hay, 1991).

Psychotic Disorders due to General Medical Conditions

There are many medical conditions that can cause psychotic symptoms. Some of these conditions directly involve the brain, such as brain tumors, seizure disorders, and infections of the brain. Others are systemic illnesses that involve many organ systems, including the brain. Some common medical causes of psychotic symptoms in the elderly are strokes, thyroid disorders, vitamin deficiencies, Parkinson's disease, inflammatory conditions, infections, and metabolic disorders. The first step in diagnosing any psychotic disorder, especially in the elderly, is to rule out a medical condition as the cause of the psychotic symptoms. Treatment of the underlying disease or condition is the key to treating these psychotic disorders. Once the underlying medical illness is treated, the psychotic symptoms often resolve. If the underlying condition cannot be treated, such as in the case of a stroke, the psychotic symptoms can often be decreased or eliminated with antipsychotic medication.

Substance-Induced Psychotic Disorder

Many drugs, both illicit and prescribed, can cause psychotic symptoms. Although illicit drug use is not usually a major problem in the elderly population, many elderly people take multiple medications that can cause them to develop a substance-induced psychotic disorder. Drugs commonly used by the elderly that can cause psychotic symptoms include anti-Parkinson's disease drugs, steroids, anticonvulsants, blood pressure and cardiac medications, antihistamines, antidepressants, and some antibiotics. Excessive use of alcohol can also cause psychotic symptoms in some older individuals. Substance-induced psychotic symptoms usually resolve when the offending drug is discontinued, although antipsychotic medication may be needed while the drug is clearing from the body or if the offending drug cannot safely be stopped.

Mood Disorders with Psychotic Features

Mood disorders have been discussed elsewhere in this chapter. In addition to the symptoms already described, major depression and bipolar disorder can present with psychotic symptoms. These symptoms are usually "mood congruent"; that is, the content of the delusions or hallucinations are appropriate to the person's mood. For example, a depressed person may hear voices telling him that he is an evil person and deserves to die, or he may have delusions that he has committed a grievous sin or has an incurable disease. A person in a manic state may have the delusion that he is the President of the United States or hear voices telling him that he has special powers. These psychotic symptoms resolve along with the other symptoms of the mood disorder when treated with medications or ECT.

Implications for Competency

Psychotic disorders can profoundly affect the capacity of an individual to make decisions. A psychotic person's thinking may be so disorganized that he or she cannot make or communicate rational decisions. Psychotic disorders impair the person's ability to distinguish external reality from intrapsychic experiences. Thus, the person may base decisions on false information generated by a disordered brain rather than on factual information. For example, a man may refuse needed surgery based on the delusion that the surgeon wants to implant a tracking device in his body so that the CIA can monitor his activities. The presence of psychosis does not automatically make a person incompetent in all areas, however. The person mentioned above may be incapable of making rational decisions regarding medical treatment but may be quite capable of managing his financial affairs and many other personal matters. In assessing the competence of a psychotic individual, it is essential to determine whether he or she is basing decisions on reality or on his or her own false beliefs and perceptions. It is also necessary to determine whether the person's thinking is organized enough to receive and evaluate information and to communicate a decision based on that information. A psychotic person's capacity to make decisions can often be restored with antipsychotic medication.

SUMMARY

Competency, the capacity for decision making, can be impaired partially or totally by psychiatric disorders. Mood disorders consist principally of depression and manic-depression. Cognitive disorders include delirium but principally the various types of dementia. Psychotic disorders result from various causes, and schizophrenia is a major type of psychotic disorder. An important aspect of mood disorders and psychotic disorders is their treatment outcomes because of the possibility of reversing decisional incapacity to decisional capacity.

REFERENCES

American Psychiatric Association (1990). The practice of electroconvulsive therapy: Recommendations for treatment, training, and privileging. *A Task Force Report of the American Psychiatric Association.* Washington, DC: American Psychiatric Association.

American Psychiatric Association (1994). *Diagnostic and statistical manual of mental disorders* (4th ed.) (DSM IV). Washington, DC, American Psychiatric Association.

Conn, J. D. K. (1991). Delirium and other organic mental disorders. In J. Sadavoy, L. Lazarus, & L. Jarvik (Eds.), *Comprehensive review of geriatric psychiatry* (pp. 311–336). Washington, DC: American Psychiatric Press.

Cooper, A. F., & Curry, A. R. (1976). The pathology of deafness in the paranoid and affective psychoses of later life. *Journal Psychosomatic Research, 20,* 97–105.

Cummings, J. L., & Benson, D. F. (1992). *Dementia: A clinical approach.* Boston: Butterworth-Heinemann.

Folstein, M. F., Folstein, S. E., & McHugh, P. R. (1975). Mini-mental-state: A practical method for grading the mental state of patients for the clinician. *Journal of Psychiatric Research, 12,* 189–198.

Harris, M. J., & Jeste, D. V. (1988). Late-onset schizophrenia: An overview. *Schizophrenia Bulletin, 14,* 39–55.

Hay, D. P. (1989). Electroconvulsive therapy in the medically ill elderly. *Convulsive Therapy*, *5*, 8–16.

Hay, D. P. (1991). Electroconvulsive therapy. In J. Sadavoy, L. Lazarus, & L. Jarvik (Eds.), *Comprehensive Review of Geriatric Psychiatry* (pp. 469–485). Washington, DC: American Psychiatric Press.

Ineichen, B. (1987). Measuring the rising tide. How many dementia cases will there be by 2001? *British Journal of Psychiatry*, *150*, 193–200.

Jeste, D. V., Manley, M., & Harris, M. J. (1991). Psychoses. In J. Sadavoy, L. Lazarus, & L. Jarvik (Eds.), *Comprehensive Review of Geriatric Psychiatry* (pp. 353–368). Washington, DC: American Psychiatric Press.

Kumar, A., & Gottlieb, G. (1993). Frontotemporal dementias: A new clinical syndrome? *American Journal of Geriatric Psychiatry*, *1*(2), 95–107.

Kupfer, D. J., Frank, E., Perel, J. M, Cornes, C., Mallinger, A. G., Thase, M. E., McEachran, A. B., & Grochocinski, V. J. (1992). Five-year outcome for maintenance therapies in recurrent depression. *Archives of General Psychiatry*, *49*, 769–773.

Mace, N. L., & Rabins, P. V. (1991). *The 36-Hour Day*. Baltimore, MD: The John Hopkins University Press.

Mulsant, B. H., Rosen, J., Thorton, J. E., & Zubenko, G. S. (1991). A prospective naturalistic study of electroconvulsive therapy in late life depression. *Journal of Geriatric Psychiatry and Neurology*, *4*, 3–13.

National Institutes of Health Consensus Conference (1992). Diagnosis and treatment of depression in late life. *Journal of the American Medical Association*, *268*, 1018–1024.

Nishimura, T., & Kobayashi, T. (1993). Scales for mental state and daily living activities for the elderly: Clinical behavioral scales for assessing demented patients. *International Psychogeriatrics*, *5*(2), 117–134.

Reisberg, B., Borenstein, J., Salob, S. P., Ferris, S. H., Franssen, S. H., & Georgotas, A. (1987). Behavioral symptoms in Alzheimer's Disease: Phenomenology and treatment. *Journal of Clinical Psychiatry*, *48*(5), 95–155.

Yesavage, J. A., Brink, T. L., Rose, T. L., Lum, O., Huang, V., Adey, M., & Leirer, V. O. (1983). Development and evaluation of a geriatric depression screening scale: A preliminary report. *Journal of Psychiatric Research*, *17*(1), 37–49.

Zubenko, G. S., Mulsant, B. H., Rifai, A. H., Sweet, R. A., Pasternak, R. E., Marino, L. J., & Tu, X. M. (1994). Impact of acute psychiatric inpatient treatment on major depression in late life and prediction of response. *American Journal of Psychiatry*, *151*(7), 987–994.

Zung, W. W. K. (1965). A self-rating depression scale. *Archives of General Psychiatry*, *12*, 63–70.

PART 3

Judicial Aspects

CHAPTER 5

Judicial Process in Guardianship Proceedings

John N. Kirkendall

Although each state has its own laws governing guardianship, many similarities exist in the proceedings that take place in courts throughout the country. A series of well-defined steps is commonly found in guardianship cases.

PETITION

The first formal step in a guardianship proceeding is the filing of a petition for guardianship with the court. In most states an interested adult and, in many states, an interested entity such as a social service agency (Zimny & Diamond, 1994) or a state agency may file a petition. The petition is a form that can be obtained from the court that appoints guardians, usually the probate court. The petitioner completes the form by requesting that a guardian be appointed for an individual, the respondent. Some courts have brochures to explain in detail the procedures to be followed in guardianship cases, and some may even have a videotape explaining the steps in the process and the duties and responsibilities of guardians and conservators. Hurme (1991) described instructional brochures for new guardians provided by courts in various states. "Typical topics include limits on guardian's authority, how to assess the ward's needs, where to obtain forms, community resources, record keeping, how to be an effective guardian and alternatives to guardianship. Filing fees, telephone numbers of where to call for information and a copy of the guardianship statute are also of value to the guardian" (p. 27). Brochures have also been developed by individuals (Fins, 1992; Rausch, 1990). Instructional materials are important because most guardians and conservators appointed by the courts are family members (Zimny, Diamond, Mau, Law, and Chung, 1997) who petitioned to have themselves appointed.

The court may require that petitioners employ the services of an attorney. Even if not required, an attorney who is experienced in guardianship matters can be helpful in filing the petition and completing the other steps in the proceedings. An attorney can be particularly helpful, even necessary, if problems arise during the guardianship proceedings. It is a signal that there are problems when the respondent is adamantly opposed to the guardianship. It is also a signal, as exemplified below, when arguments arise among siblings concerning guardianship for their mother.

   (a) Is the guardianship necessary?
      "Mother is perfectly capable of deciding that for herself."
   (b) Who should be the guardian and the conservator?
      "I would never trust my brother Bob with our mother's money."
   (c) Should there be co-guardians and co-conservators?
      "I don't want all that responsibility myself, but I wouldn't mind helping my sister."
      "My brother and I could never work together on anything important."
      "I would never trust what those two would think of."
   (d) Where should the respondent live?
      "Mom just can't live safely by herself any more."
      "My sister can't take proper care of her."
      "A nursing home would just kill her."
   (e) What medical treatment should the respondent have?
      "Mom is not able to understand or evaluate the medical alternatives available to her."
      "My brothers and I can't agree upon the necessity for the surgery."

To find an attorney who deals in guardianship cases, call the local or state bar association.

The petition is a very important document because the answers given to the questions in the petition provide essential information to the court about the problem and the people involved. Most petitions will require the following information:

(a) What is the name and address of the respondent?
(b) How is the respondent acting that causes you to believe that he or she needs a guardian? Why can't the respondent make decisions without a guardian?
(c) What are some specific things the respondent is doing that show the need for help.
   "She left home last night and couldn't find her way home."
   "He tried to cook dinner last night. He left the burners on the stove on high with very little food in the pan. He then went outside. Serious smoke damage to the house resulted. The neighbors called the fire department."
   "She ordered a new car but hasn't driven in several years. She has no driver's license."
   "He has an unexplained body lump. His physician believes it is potentially life threatening. He refuses to consent to a biopsy and says that God will take care of him."
(d) What decisions need to be made for the respondent that he or she is unable to make? These typically fall into one or more of three categories: medical, housing, and financial.
(e) Who are the members of the respondent's family?
(f) What property and assets does the respondent have?
(g) Is there a power of attorney in effect? Who holds the power?
(h) What is the name and address of the suggested guardian? Has the person agreed to serve?
(i) Is there a person who has been appointed to receive social security benefits or veteran's benefits on the respondent's behalf? What are the person's name and address?
(j) Who has been providing the care for the respondent in the past few months?
(k) Has the respondent nominated anyone to perform the duties of a guardian in other documents, other than a power of attorney, such as a trust?

The petitioner files the completed petition at the court. A filing fee will probably be charged at that time, and certain other expenses may have to be paid to the court after the petition is filed. These can include the cost of an investigation, a medical evaluation of the respondent, and attorney's fees for an attorney appointed by the court for the respondent. If the petition is granted, the court costs can usually be paid or reimbursed from the ward's assets. The court where the petition is to be filed will be happy to explain its procedure for assessing fees and costs.

NOTICE OF HEARING

A hearing will be scheduled by the court at the time the petition is filed. The hearing date will be set within 60 days of the date the petition is filed, and often much sooner.

There are certain people who are entitled to receive notice of the hearing. Those people must receive papers in the mail or in person telling them that a guardianship petition has been filed, what the petitioner is requesting from the court, and when the hearing will be held. In some states, the court will notify the proper persons. In other states, the responsibility for proper service (notification) is on the person who files the petition. The court will indicate the required procedure when the petition is filed.

EMERGENCY GUARDIANSHIP

There are occasions when the usual time lines for guardianship cannot be followed. These are cases in which the risk of harm to the respondent is imminent. In Florida, the court can appoint an emergency temporary guardian, but the statute requires that "the court must specifically find that there appears to be an imminent danger that the physical or mental health or safety of the person will be seriously impaired or that his property is in danger of being wasted, misappropriated or lost unless immediate action is taken" (Rausch, 1990, p. 28). For example, if it is believed that an emergency medical procedure is necessary for the respondent and the respondent refuses to consent but lacks the capacity to make an informed decision, a petition for emergency guardianship may be filed.

State laws and procedures vary in key principles in emergency guardianships. Not all states require an attorney for a respondent in this circumstance, and they may not require an investigation on such short notice. In addition, notice requirements are usually shortened and fewer individuals may need to be notified.

Because of constitutional considerations, the court will attempt to adhere as closely as possible to nonemergency procedures in the emergency situation. It is essential that the respondent be notified. It is good practice to make every effort to hold the hearing in the presence of the respondent. An attorney should represent the respondent at the hearing. In addition, as much notice to as many persons who would receive it under nonemergency circumstances should be attempted. The investigation may have to be abbreviated because of the emergent circumstances but should not be done away with altogether.

Special emphasis is given to following due process in emergency cases for two reasons. First, a court may be inclined to do only what the state law requires. The law of some states, however, predates recent federal cases that suggest that following the minimum standards specified in the state law may not be constitutionally sufficient. For example, state law may not require personal service on a respondent in emergency cases, whereas federal case law requires it. Second, emergency guardianships are often requested to enable action to be taken that cannot be undone, such as amputation. If persons don't receive notice, an attorney is not appointed for the respondent, or an investigation is not conducted, then the court may not be made aware of factors critical to its decision about granting or denying the petition for an emergency guardianship.

Sometimes the action requested in an emergency petition is to move the respondent into a nursing home. This is seldom an emergency of the kind that requires that notice, attorneys, and investigations be sacrificed in favor of speed. Once an older person has gone through the trauma of a move, a second move may be very unwise—even if a better place to live is found before a full hearing is convened.

COURT INVESTIGATION

The court usually appoints an individual to conduct an investigation to be completed before the guardianship hearing (see Court Staff in chapter 6). This investigation is one of the most important parts of the guardianship proceeding. The person who conducts the investigation is known by different names in different states. In some states, the investigator is called a *guardian ad litem*, whereas in others, he or she is a "visitor" or an "investigator." The name *guardian ad litem* is unfortunate because the *guardian ad litem* is not a guardian at all but is an investigator for the court. Gottlich and Wood (1989) reported that court investigators in California included "psychologists, social workers, gerontologists, nurses, probation officers, former conservators, and others" (p. 427).

The court investigator is responsible for making recommendations to the court. The recommendations concern granting or denying the guardianship, what powers the guardian should have, who should be the guardian, how long the guardianship should last, and the necessity of an independent evaluation of the respondent. In states where attorneys are not required for every respondent, the court investigator will recommend whether an attorney should be appointed. In other words, the investigator will have something to say about each of the major issues that will come up at the hearing.

The recommendations of the court investigator are made after interviewing a number of people. Under optimum circumstances, the investigator will talk with the respondent, the person who is the proposed guardian, the family members who are closest to the person, the neighbors, care givers, social workers, and physicians or nurses. If the proposed guardian wants to transfer the respondent to a nursing home, a visit to the home may also be important. Under difficult medical circumstances, such as where amputation or withdrawal of life support systems is being contemplated, there may also be meetings with a hospital ethics committee to determine whether the choices that are being suggested by the proposed guardian are appropriate. Such meetings will also assist the investigator in deciding whether the proposed guardian is the appropriate person to be appointed. Everyone interested in the guardianship proceeding can benefit from maximum participation in the investigation.

The investigator is often trained to recommend services as alternatives to guardianship, if these haven't been considered up to this time. For example, mediation services may be available in the community that will allow families to resolve their differences without going to court to seek guardianship. An investigator can assist the parties in engaging these services.

It is important that the court investigator hear the views of family members, friends, and care providers on the case before the investigator files the recommendations with the court. To make sure their views are heard, they can call the court within a few days after the petition is filed, find out the name and telephone number of the person serving as the investigator, and call him or her. As a result, the investigator can consider their points of view before the final recommendations are prepared and delivered to the court. The importance of such action can hardly be overstated.

COMPETENCY ASSESSMENTS

There are two principal issues that the courts in most states address at a guardianship hearing. The first of these is the issue of competency (see chapters 3 and 7). To the extent that there is incompetency, the court will determine what tasks a guardian should be authorized to perform on behalf of the respondent. In many states, there is a requirement that the court give the guardian as few powers over the respondent as possible. A competency assessment will assist the court in designing the court order that assigns to the guardian appropriate powers in each case.

In order to be valuable to the court, the assessment should be performed by a person or a team having the appropriate expertise (see chapter 3). This expertise should be in the area of the alleged cause of the disputed legal disability. For example, if mental illness is the reason for the alleged incompetency, a different evaluator may be called for than if the reason is a closed head injury. The court often has a list of experts who are available to conduct evaluations. It is usually the right of the respondents to choose their own evaluators, if they wish to do so. A family member does not have that right.

Many times professional persons are reluctant to become involved in contested court cases. A principal reason is that an appearance in court can often take up an unpredictable amount of professional time. There are two ways this can be avoided. First, arrangements can be made with the court for a specific date and time for the professional person to appear. As a result, the professional can plan ahead without sacrificing other appointments. A second way is to schedule to have the professional person's testimony taken out of court under circumstances that will allow for its admission as evidence when the case comes up for a hearing. This latter method involves the use of a deposition (written statement by a witness for use in court in his or her absence). Depositions have the advantage of taking and preserving expert testimony in a setting and at a time convenient for the professional person. Depositions have the drawback of being an additional expense that may not be affordable or merited in many guardianship cases. In cases in which deposition testimony is believed to be important, the use of an attorney is wise.

The report of the evaluator should be filed so that the court can see it before or at the time of the hearing (see chapter 7). Generally, rules of evidence would prevent a judge from relying on such a report because it is hearsay. That is, the report is written by a person not in court for the purpose of proving an issue before the court. Many courts, however, have special rules in guardianship hearings that permit the reports to be introduced as evidence. Under these circumstances, the respondent usually has the right to subpoena the preparer of the report to be present at the hearing, if questioning of the preparer is desired. The subpoena power under this rule is very seldom used. The evaluation often serves a useful purpose. If there is a difference of opinion between the petitioner and the respondent about the necessity for a guardianship, the report of the independent evaluator often provides a resolution that both parties can agree on so that on the date of the hearing everything flows very smoothly.

HEARING

Everything that has been done up to this time has been done in anticipation of the hearing. What the hearing will be like differs not only among the states but also among the counties or political subdivisions in a state. The nature of the hearing is apt to reflect the attitude of the court (judge or judges) as much as the statutes and laws by which the court is governed. People who are expected to be participants in such hearings should consider sitting in on a hearing or two before the date of the scheduled hearing in which they are interested. This will help give them a feel for the way things are done in that court. Even if an attorney has explained what transpires at a hearing, visits beforehand serve to take away any surprise element when the date of the hearing finally arrives. If prior visits are not possible and an attorney has not explained the hearing, a telephone call can be made to the court staff. While court personnel are prohibited from giving legal advice, they can describe the general procedures at the guardianship hearing.

Respondents generally have a right to a jury trial. Except for very few states, however, guardianship cases rarely are tried before a jury. In a jurisdiction where jury trials are usual, an attorney will probably be necessary.

How long does a hearing take? Many courts handle several guardianship cases in the course of a single morning, if the proceedings are uncontested. Contested cases are rare. Bulcroft, Kielkopf, & Tripp (1991) reported that none of 56 cases of guardianship of the elderly was formally contested. If there is a contest, the court may require a new date to be set for a hearing at which all witnesses can plan to be present. In a contested case, it is advisable for an attorney to check with the court in advance of the date of hearing to see if the court will be able to take the time to hear all witnesses on the scheduled date. This check is very helpful if witnesses include people traveling some distance to the hearing, expert witnesses, or persons who find it difficult to travel because of physical or other reasons. It is also expensive to miss work, particularly if the hearing is going to be rescheduled on another day for which time from work will also have to be taken.

What witnesses will the court expect to be present at a hearing? In all courts, the person who files the petition is expected to appear. The person who is the nominated guardian should also be present. Whether the respondent has to be there is a question of state law, but it is preferred. The respondent has a right to be present. In fact, some courts feel strongly enough about allowing a respondent to be present that if he or she wishes hearings are moved to the respondent's hospital room, nursing home, or residence. If someone is aware that the respondent wants to be present, the court should be informed so that it can plan to make arrangements, if possible, to move the site of the hearing. This will probably require a new hearing date to be set.

Some courts may require the expert who prepared the competency assessment to be present. Others will be content to simply read the report, unless the expert is subpoenaed by the respondent. Anyone who opposes the petition should plan to be present to explain his or her opposition. There may also be witnesses who can testify as to the respondent's abilities to do some or all of the tasks for which a guardian is being sought.

The Americans with Disabilities Act applies to courts. The Act requires the court to make reasonable accommodations for persons with disabilities. If a person interested in the court proceeding has a disability, the court should be notified reasonably in advance of the hearing about steps to take in order to make the person's participation more effective and rewarding. Accommodations can often be made to assist those with hearing, sight, mobility, or language familiarity needs.

What are the major issues to be decided at the hearing? First, is the respondent able to receive and process information? A competency assessment will address that issue, but there may not be a competency assessment in many cases. If not, testimony will be taken from someone familiar with the respondent. That testimony should indicate to what extent the respondent understands the consequences of the decisions made. Ideally, the court is not particularly interested in the values of the respondent, that is, whether the court would make the same choices with the same available information. The question is whether the respondent is able to think a matter through and develop a conclusion based on values important to the respondent.

The second issue is one of need. A respondent may be completely incompetent to decide life's questions, but it may be unnecessary for anyone to be appointed to make those decisions for him or her because all needs are being met. This can be a very important defense, if a respondent is resisting guardianship. (See chapter 7 for a more detailed discussion of judicial decisions concerning competency and need.) Other issues at the hearing are the identity of the guardian, the duties the guardian will assume, whether a bond will be required and in what amount, how long the guardianship will last, and whether a date for review of the guardianship should be established.

Once a hearing has been concluded, the court enters orders. It is often said a court speaks through its orders. That simply means that the results of a court proceeding are contained in orders signed by the judge. Some courts prepare the required guardianship orders at the end of the hearing and will either hand them to the appropriate person after the hearing is over or will mail them. Other courts will require the prevailing party to prepare the required orders. Orders appointing a guardian or conservator, or both, are important papers because the nursing home, hospital, physician, bank, trust officers, and others want to see official proof of the authority of the guardian and/or conservator to make decisions on the ward's behalf.

Before leaving court, a newly appointed guardian or conservator, or both, should be sure to understand the duties assigned by the court. In some states, the conservator appointed to make decisions about a ward's finances will have to file a bond with the court and then file an inventory of the ward's assets. Until the appropriate bond is filed, the orders of appointment are not issued by the judge, and the conservator has no authority to act. A guardian and a conservator may be required to file an annual report of the personal and financial condition of the ward (see chapter 9). The court staff can provide the required report forms, which will indicate what information and records must be provided to the court later. It is highly advisable for the guardian and conservator to keep detailed information throughout the reporting period for use in preparing the necessary reports. Failure to file reports on time will trigger a note from the court stating that reports are due. Further, failure to file could result in removal of the person whose duty it is to file or in contempt charges being brought against the offending person.

RESTORATION OF WARD

The trend in guardianship laws is to require the guardian to use all reasonable means to restore the ward to a state of full functioning. This is a laudable, if often unobtainable, objective. For example, an Alzheimer's patient whose prognosis is steady and certain deterioration is not amenable to such restoration. On the other hand, a closed head injury victim or a person with alcoholism may be rehabilitated. It is the duty of the court and the guardian to devise a plan to promote optimal functioning of the ward. Creative, but above all involved and interested, persons can investigate and put into effect plans to help wards achieve their highest level of functioning. The value of a guardianship arrangement to a ward is usually directly related to the amount of time and interest a guardian is able to supply to the ward. If a guardian has been appointed by the court mainly to file state-mandated paperwork, the guardianship is a rather limited endeavor. The ultimate measure of a successful guardianship is the service the guardian is able to provide to the ward. Paperwork should merely be a reflection of the service and not the purpose of the guardianship.

TERMINATION OF THE GUARDIANSHIP

For elderly wards, the principle reason guardianships are terminated is death of the ward. Guardianships are also terminated by the court for other reasons, such as a request by the guardian or conservator to be released of the responsibility of serving the ward or failure of the guardian or conservator to comply with statutory and court requirements. Zimny et al. (1997) reported that of 61 cases of guardianship of the elderly that were terminated over a 6-year period, 52 ended due to death of the ward, 8 due to depletion of the wards' assets, and 1 due to the ward moving out of the court's jurisdiction.

Guardianships are terminated when the ward returns to a state of functioning that permits the ward to process information sufficiently to make informed decisions. But termination in such cases is not automatic. It requires a process similar to that for establishing the guardianship. If termination seems appropriate, a petition to the court will initiate the proceedings. The ward or others on the ward's behalf can request such termination. There are cases when the ward who is the subject of a guardianship proceeding moves out of state. This will necessitate termination of the guardianship in the originating state. If a new guardian is being sought in the ward's new state of residence, the state where the initial guardianship was established should be notified.

MODIFICATION OF GUARDIANSHIP

An intermediate step to termination is modification. If a ward acquires the ability to make certain kinds of decisions, the guardianship powers can and should be modified. This may be important as a part of the therapy of a ward who is struggling to regain autonomy. A court should be mindful in its original order to consider a review date if the case appears to be one in which a return to full functioning is reasonably likely. Small increments of additional power returned to the ward may seem insignificant at first, but they are not insignificant to the ward. When brought to the attention of the court, the court will be pleased to reflect the ward's improved functioning in the guardianship order. Likewise, deterioration in a ward's condition may cause the order to be modified to place more powers in the hands of the guardian.

RESIGNATION OF GUARDIAN

A guardian or conservator may wish to resign. The tasks may become burdensome, the health of the guardian may decline, the ward may move to a different county, the guardian may retire to another state, and so on. A petition for discharge should be filed with the court, and a hearing will be scheduled. The guardian will be thanked and excused by court order upon filing a final report. It is always helpful to the court if a successor guardian can be suggested who is acceptable to the ward, but this is not a requirement. A guardian or conservator who has provided faithful service to the ward should not be required to find a willing successor who is agreeable to all interested parties before the discharge is granted.

SUMMARY

Alternatives to guardianship should be explored in advance of requesting guardianship for a person. If alternatives do not exist, a guardianship can usually be in place within 60 days of the date of petitioning. If there is an emergency, it can be much faster. A court will try to limit the duties of the guardian and conservator based on the abilities of the ward so that the ward retains as many rights as possible. In order for a guardianship to be successful, the guardian should be prepared to spend time with the ward and cause the ward to receive services based on the special needs of the particular ward being served.

REFERENCES

Bulcroft, K., Kielkopf, M. R., & Tripp, K. (1991). Elderly wards and their legal guardians: Analysis of county probate records in Ohio and Washington. *The Gerontologist, 31*(2), 156–164.

Fins, D. L. (1992). *Serving as guardian or conservator: A guide for agencies and individuals.* Worcester, MA: Jewish Family Service of Worcester, Inc.

Gottlich, V. & Wood, E. (1989). Statewide review of guardianships: The California and Maryland approaches. *Clearinghouse Review*, Special Issue, Summer.

Hurme, S. (1991). *Steps to enhance guardianship monitoring.* Washington, DC: American Bar Association.

Rausch, I. (1990). *A practical guide to guardianship.* Palm Harbor, FL: Pine Cone Publishing.

Zimny, G. H. & Diamond, J. A. (1994). *Social service agencies as guardians of elderly wards.* St. Louis: St. Louis University.

Zimny, G. H., Diamond, J. A, Mau, M. M., Law, A. C. K., & Chung, C. (1997). Six-year longitudinal study of finances of elderly wards under guardianship. *The Journal of Ethics, Law, and Aging, 3(2),* 91–101.

CHAPTER 6

The Courts

Field C. Benton

PROBATE COURTS

Name

Most people assume that guardianship cases are one of the things that probate judges handle in probate court. These folks are correct—up to a point. But in more than half the states, probate judges work in courts labeled as something other than probate court.

Twenty states and the District of Columbia have limited jurisdiction courts or have divisions of the general jurisdiction courts with the word probate as a part of their official names. In New York and New Jersey these are called surrogate court. As their names suggest, limited jurisdiction courts can handle only certain kinds of cases and those in which a maximum amount of money is at stake. General jurisdiction courts can handle all kinds of cases without regard to the dollar amounts in dispute.

Table 6.1 contains the name of the "guardianship court" in each state and each possession. Basically speaking, courts dealing with guardianship cases fall structurally into four categories:

1. Eleven states have formal probate courts statewide (Alabama, Arkansas, Connecticut, Georgia, Maine, Michigan, New Hampshire, New Mexico, Rhode Island, South Carolina, and Vermont).

TABLE 6.1 Names of the Courts Handling Guardianship Cases

State	Name of the Court	State	Name of the Court
Alabama	Probate Court	Mississippi	Chancery Court
Alaska	Superior Court	Missouri	Circuit Court
Arizona	Superior Court	Montana	District Court
Arkansas	Chancery Probate Court	Nebraska	County Court
		Nevada	District Court
California	Superior Court (Probate Division)	New Hampshire	Probate Court
		New Jersey	Surrogate Court
Colorado	Probate Court (in Denver), elsewhere District Court	New Mexico	District Court or, in some localities, County Court
		New York	Surrogate's Court
Connecticut	Probate Court	North Carolina	Superior Court
Delaware	Court of Chancery	North Dakota	County Court
District of Columbia	Superior Court (Probate Division)	Ohio	Court of Common Pleas or, in some localities, Probate Court
Florida	Circuit Court		
Georgia	Probate Court	Oklahoma	District Court
Hawaii	Circuit Court or Family Court	Oregon	Circuit Court
		Pennsylvania	Court of Common Pleas (Orphans Division)
Idaho	District Court		
Illinois	Circuit Court		
Indiana	Probate Court	Rhode Island	Probate Court
Iowa	Probate Court	South Carolina	Probate Court
Kansas	District Court	South Dakota	Circuit Court
Kentucky	Circuit Court	Tennessee	Probate Court
Louisiana	District Court	Texas	Probate Court
Maine	Probate Court	Utah	District Court
Maryland	Orphan Court or Circuit Court	Vermont	Probate Court
		Virginia	Circuit Court
Massachusetts	Probate Court or Family Court	Washington	Superior Court
		West Virginia	Circuit Court
Michigan	Probate Court	Wisconsin	Circuit Court
Minnesota	District Court	Wyoming	District Court

NOTE: Since state guardianship statutes are subject to revision, it might be prudent to confirm the name of the court as listed here.

2. Two states and a federal district have probate divisions or probate departments permanently created by law as a part of a general jurisdiction court (Massachusetts and Missouri and the District of Columbia).
3. Five states have mixed, or differing, probate court structures and organization created by law, depending on the region of the state in which that court is located (Colorado, Indiana, Ohio, Tennessee, and Texas).
4. Thirty-two states have no formal, permanent probate court as such. These states usually have a probate department within the general jurisdiction trial court that is established internally by the court itself rather than being permanently established by state law. Civil, criminal, and domestic relations departments might also exist within that court system (for example, as in Arizona, California, and Minnesota).

Hours

In some states, the court handling guardianships may not be open for business on a full-time basis. Hours open is something that can vary in each local court. For example, if the judge is a part-time judge, it may be that the court is open only half days or perhaps only a few days each week. On the other hand, most courts are open during normal business hours on every weekday.

As an added complication, due to shrinking budgets and limited staffing, many courts have been forced to somewhat foreshorten the hours during which pleadings (legal papers relating to a case) can be filed and may lack full staffs.

The clerk of court can be contacted for information about a court's business hours.

JUDGES

Depending on the laws of each state, there are persons with different qualifications who may act as the judge who conducts the guardianship hearing.

The judge probably is a full-time judge who practiced law for at least 5 years before becoming a judge. In some places, however, the judge might be a practicing lawyer who also is a part-time judge (Connecticut has this system) while in other places the judge might be a nonlawyer serving part-time as a probate judge (as in parts of Georgia, Maryland, and South Carolina).

Furthermore, in some large metropolitan areas, there is another judicial official variously called a *magistrate, referee, commissioner,* or *hearing officer* depending on the state. This official functions like a judge in deciding routine cases in which a court order is sought (to appoint a guardian, to instruct the guardian upon request, etc.) based on witnesses testifying under oath and other evidence and as to which all interested parties have been given formal notification or "notice" a specified time in advance of that hearing. In many instances, guardians are appointed by this official. If either the petitioner or the proposed ward objects to the quasi judge procedure, however, or if a basic issue is contested, the judge will conduct the hearing.

In other states, if the guardianship hearing turns into a contested trial, either questioning the *need* for a guardianship or quarreling over *who* ought to become guardian, a nonlawyer judge will simply transfer the case up to the next higher trial court in that state's system. Sometimes this is done routinely in states having part-time probate courts. Thus, as a general rule, the truly controversial and contested guardianship trials are conducted by a skilled full-time judge.

As an aside, it's important to remember that regardless of background and perhaps limited legal training, all probate judges are peers when exercising their official judicial duties and all are entitled to due respect and courtesy from the parties, counsel, and witnesses.

COURT STAFF

The size of the court staff varies widely depending on the nature and caliber of the court. As a bare minimum, all courts have a clerk of court who is assisted in larger courts by one or more deputy clerks. Other staff members include a division clerk, a court visitor, a bailiff, a court reporter, and a law clerk.

The *deputy court clerk* will be the first person encountered in the process of commencing a guardianship proceeding. The guardianship petition is filed with the deputy court clerk, and ultimately the clerk will issue the Letters of Guardianship, an official document proving the person named in the Letters is indeed the court-appointed guardian for the ward.

The *clerk of court* or a deputy clerk will be in the court's front office or at a public counter prominently identified on the door as the Clerk of Court's office. In large courts, the clerk of court is akin to the office manager, and the deputy clerks are the ones dealing with the general public.

Many people seek to establish a guardianship without asking for a lawyer's help, and that certainly is permissible. The process is called "acting *pro se*" which means literally "for one's self." Persons choosing to act *pro se* cannot expect to get legal advice from any of the court staff. Court clerks are not lawyers, and it is unfair for a person to ask a court clerk to practice law for the person's benefit. There is a very fine line between a court clerk giving general advice about such things as the needed pleadings forms to be used or the general procedures to be followed and the clerk giving an opinion about how the laws apply to the facts in a particular case.

In most states, there is a specific law prohibiting court employees from giving legal advice. In the real world, most court clerks do more along that line than they would wish their boss, the judge, to know about!

The next member of the court staff likely to be encountered is the *division clerk*, who is like a secretary for the judge. The division clerk usually is in a separate room, adjacent to the judge's chambers (the judge's private office). It is usually the division clerk who maintains the court calendar, called the docket, which is a list of scheduled trials and hearings, and who gives persons the date and time for guardianship hearings.

In very small courts, the judge has no division clerk and makes the trial settings as part of the judicial function. In a few courts (some of which actually are located in the judge's own home!), the judge's spouse serves as court clerk/division clerk, thus augmenting the family income.

Depending on the state's laws, a *court visitor* or *court investigator* (see chapters 5 and 9) appointed by the court may take action between the time the guardianship petition is filed and the date of the hearing. One of this person's functions is to interview the prospective ward and to explain the proceedings, the consequences if a guardian is appointed, and the prospective ward's legal rights. The court visitor also interviews the petitioner, ward's physician (if one is involved), nursing home staff (if the ward resides in a nursing home), and other "interested parties." Prior to the hearing, this impartial investigator makes a written report to the court, thereby acting, as some say, "as the eyes and ears of the court." This report is available to all parties. It often helps put the case in proper perspective because it is an evaluation of the facts by a disinterested third person. Court visitors are often salaried members of the court staff, but, increasingly, they are apt to be well-trained volunteers.

At a time when the public funds appropriated for courts become less and less, more and more courts are looking to trained volunteers for help in providing investigator and other services that we all have come to expect from our courts. In chapter 9, Hurme describes a highly successful and expanding program for volunteer court visitors and court auditors and records researchers who are trained to help courts monitor and audit guardianship cases. Hurme (1990–91) describes four programs that select and train persons to serve as guardians in cases for which they are needed by the court. In two of the programs, the persons serve as volunteer guardians. Rogers (1994) provides a description of several other volunteer guardian programs. Interested persons can inquire at their local probate court about these important opportunities for volunteers to help. The day is coming soon for all courts when it will be only with the help of volunteers that the courts can continue to function as well as one might wish in terms of properly coping with guardianships.

Court staffs often include others such as file clerks, auditors, and data processors who are important to the court's operation. Two other court staff members, both of whom work in the courtroom itself, are the bailiff and the court reporter. Their functions are discussed in the next section.

Some judges are assisted by a *law clerk*, who usually is a law school student working part-time. The law clerk does such things as checking files for completeness prior to trial, helping the judge with legal research, drafting legal memos for the judge, and performing other helpful minor tasks.

COURTROOMS

Most guardianship hearings are held in the typical traditional courtroom, which has usually been rather accurately depicted in various TV programs. A skeletal floor plan of a typical courtroom is presented in Figure 6.1.

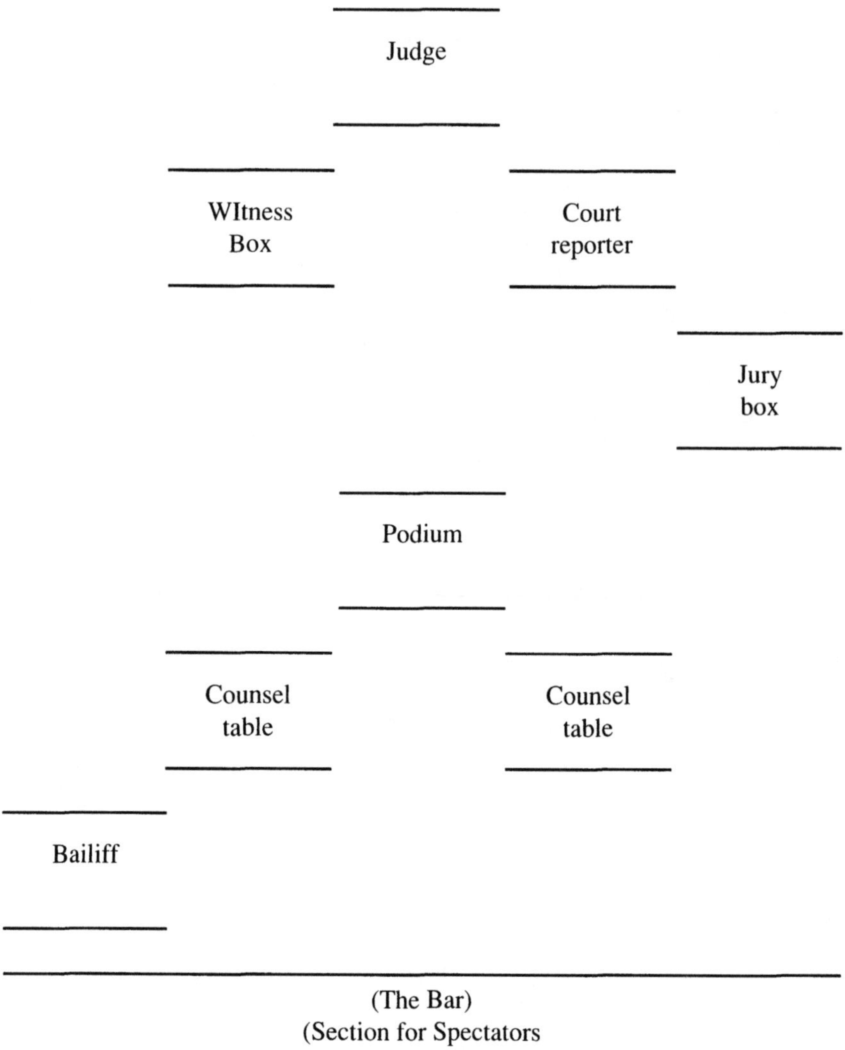

———————

Judge

———————

——————— ———————

WItness   Court
Box   reporter

——————— ———————

———————

Jury
box

———————

———————

Podium

———————

——————— ———————

Counsel   Counsel
table   table

——————— ———————

———————

Bailiff

———————

————————————————————————

(The Bar)
(Section for Spectators

FIGURE 6.1 Floor plan of a typical courtroom.

Seated behind a massive elevated desk (the bench) at the front of the courtroom is *the judge*, whose task it is to conduct the trial, to consider the evidence, to decide if a guardianship should be created, and to determine who the guardian should be and what powers the guardian should have. Traditionally, judges wear black robes to set them apart from the other participants in the trial and to symbolize the solemnity and objective detachment of the judicial role.

The witness box or *witness stand* is at one corner of the bench, and *the court reporter* is at another corner. The witness box is usually an elevated enclosure with a comfortable reclining swivel chair and, often, a microphone to ensure that the witness's testimony is clearly heard.

The court reporter's task is to record all that is said and done during a trial so that there will be an accurate and complete record of the proceedings. The reporter ordinarily uses a special kind of machine to transcribe the testimony, although in some courts this is done by tape recording.

There are two separate counsel (lawyer) tables, one for each side of the case. In a guardianship hearing, the petitioner and the petitioner's lawyer will sit at one table and the respondent and the respondent's lawyer will sit at the other table. The question of who sits at which table is either a matter of local custom or the choice of whoever arrives at court first on that day. Judges don't care who sits where.

Midway between the counsel tables and the bench is a *podium* of some sort, a stand-up desk, usually equipped with a microphone, from which the lawyers speak. Most judges expect the lawyers to stay very near the podium and not roam around as they question witnesses or address the jury. This is particularly important in older, large courtrooms where microphones are essential. As a matter of custom and courtesy, lawyers wishing to hand something to a witness (often, an exhibit presented as evidence) will ask the judge, "May I approach the witness?" before leaving the podium.

The *jury box* can be on either side of a courtroom. It, too, is enclosed and has 12 comfortable reclining swivel chairs arranged in two rows of 6 each. The back row is elevated, as in a stadium, to provide a clear view for the 6 jurors in that row. In many states, a jury of 6 decides civil cases, including guardianships, and juries of 12 are used only in criminal cases. Not all states permit jury trials for guardianship proceedings, however. (Although my home state of Colorado does permit such a jury trial without payment of a jury fee, in my 12 years as a probate judge, I've never conducted a single one.)

A railing separates the front part of the courtroom from the rows of benches provided for spectators. This railing is called *the bar*, and only lawyers and their clients are permitted to be inside that railing. Being permitted inside the railing generated the familiar phrase admitted to the bar and also generated the description of lawyers who have successfully passed "the bar examination" as "members of the bar." Often there is a row of chairs inside and along the Bar for visiting lawyers to occupy while waiting.

The *bailiff* is seated at the entrance of the bar railing and, depending on local custom, may be either a layperson or a uniformed deputy sheriff. The bailiff's job is to maintain order, to usher witnesses in, to oversee the jury, and to perform other similar duties. The bailiff also announces the opening and closing of the court session, often with a formalized announcement such as, "Please rise. Hear ye, hear ye, hear ye, the Probate Court is now in session, the Honorable Oliver Wendell Holmes presiding. Be seated!"

In some courts, the bailiff swears in the witnesses. I prefer to do that myself, simply to establish eye contact and rapport with the witness whose testimony I'll soon be weighing.

Not all guardianship cases are conducted in courtrooms. In some states, these trials customarily take place in more intimate, informal settings such as around a conference table or in the judge's chambers. Wherever it is held, it is essential that the basic format includes sworn testimony presented to an objective fact finder, the opportunity to cross-examine witnesses, and an accurate verbatim record of the proceedings. Of overriding importance is to have a "fair trial." The place in which the trial is held is of lesser importance. On rare occasions, I've conducted a guardianship hearing in a nursing home cafeteria (otherwise empty, of course) or a hospital conference room, always taking care to wear my judicial robe for whatever effect it may have on the participants.

In guardianship hearings, although the trial is held in open court, I sometimes take testimony from the respondent in the informal and relaxed surroundings of my chambers with the court reporter, the lawyers, and usually the petitioner present. Courtrooms can be terrifying for elderly persons. One of them even had a heart attack—a mild one, fortunately—while in the witness box in my courtroom.

GUARDIANSHIP APPEALS

As in any other kind of civil litigation, parties in a guardianship trial can appeal the decision of the trial court. Just who has the legal status to initiate an appeal is a technical matter of law, but generally it could be either the petitioner or the ward.

An appeal is an expensive and time-consuming process. The person appealing (the appellant) must file the appeal in a court of review, the appellate court, established especially to consider appeals from the trial courts. The appellate documents designate the reasons for the appeal and the parts of the guardianship trial court transcript involving those points. The appellant will order a transcript of the relevant portions of the trial court proceedings from the court reporter to attach to the appellate documents. The party against whom the appeal is taken is called the appellee. Sometimes the appellee will submit additional relevant portions of the transcript for the appellate court to consider.

Generally speaking, the appeal can be based only on alleged mistakes of law made by the trial judge or on procedural irregularities. A "mistake of law" would occur if a judge allowed improper evidence such as second-hand hearsay testimony about a respondent's infirmities, for instance. It would be a "procedural irregularity" to conduct the trial on a specified day if the respondent had not been properly provided with the required advance formal notification of that date, time, and place of the trial. Ordinarily, the appellate court will not overturn the trial court's findings of fact if there is evidence in the trial transcript to support those facts. Simply being disappointed over the decision by the trial court is not grounds for an appeal.

The parties to the appeal must file legal briefs describing their positions in detail. After the appellate court has reviewed these briefs, the parties will have an opportunity to present oral arguments in the appellate court. Several months later, the appellate court will hand down a written decision.

The appellate court's decision will either

1. uphold the trial court;
2. reverse the trial court and send the case back with instructions about what the trial court should do to rectify its error(s); or
3. a combination of these, namely, upholding the trial court in part and reversing that court's decision in part. In that event, the case might need to come back to the trial court for further action.

Because of the large number of cases being appealed, this appellate decision probably will be handed down two years or more after the trial was completed. That delay is one reason for there being so few appeals in guardianship cases.

Several years ago, however, there was an appeal from one of my decisions (with my blessings) challenging what then was the part of our state's guardianship law that stated that the need for a guardianship had to be proven only by "a preponderance" of the evidence rather than by "clear and convincing" evidence. In my decision, I specifically mentioned that I was utilizing a "preponderance of evidence" standard of proof, thus deliberately setting the stage for this appeal.

A "preponderance" of the evidence simply means proof that a fact is "more likely than not" whereas "clear and convincing" evidence is proof that a fact is highly probable and free from serious or substantial doubt. In a matter involving such grave consequences as a guardianship, I believed that the supporting facts should be proven by evidence that was highly probable and free from serious or substantial doubt, even though Colorado law did not require that higher degree of proof. As I had hoped, the appellate court sent the case back to me for retrial on the basis that a recent federal case had held that the stricter burden of proof should have been applied in guardianships. A few months later, our State Legislature took note of that appellate decision and amended our guardianship laws to require this stricter burden of proof be met.

Examples of appeals in guardianship cases can be found in the *Mental Health Law Reporter*. The January, 1997, issue contained three such cases (Guardianship briefs, 1997). The appellate court upheld the decision of the trial court in a Colorado case and also in a Texas case but reversed it in an Oregon case. The three cases, in order, dealt with award of attorney fees, sale of a ward's property, and changing beneficiaries on annuity policies of a deceased ward.

Most states continue to "fine-tune" the procedures in guardianship cases. The legislature may limit the powers of a guardian so as to meet the individual needs of the ward, require ongoing monitoring of existing guardianships, require filing of a "guardianship plan" early in the guardianship, simplify the process for asking that a guardianship be ended, and otherwise protect the rights of those for whom a guardianship is needed. As one example, Wank (1997) briefly described two new guardianship amendments passed in 1996 by the Illinois General Assembly. One amendment expanded the list of activities that courts may allow a guardian of the estate to undertake. Eleven new powers were added to the list. The other amendment provided legal protection from liability for guardians.

SUMMARY

Guardianship cases require a court. It may be a probate court or may go by another name. The court staff can range from one part-time clerk to a number of different types of clerks. The court may have one part-time judge or a number of full-time judges hearing guardianship cases. The cases are ordinarily heard in the courtroom but can be heard in quite different settings. The appellate court hears appeals of decisions made in the trial court.

REFERENCES

Guardianship briefs. (1997, January). *Mental Health Law Reporter*, *15*(1), 7–8.
Hurme, S. B. (1990–91, Winter). Programs address need for qualified guardians. *Bifocal*, *15*(4), 1–4.
Rogers, A. (1994, September). In search of volunteer guardians. *Shepard's Elder Care/Law Newsletter*, *4*(7), 1–10.
Wank, J. H. (1997, Winter). Developments in Illinois guardianship law. *National Guardian*, *10*(1), 9–10.

CHAPTER 7

Judicial Decisions in Guardianship Cases

James Brock

In most states, it is very rare for a guardianship case to be heard by a jury. In nonjury guardianship cases, the judge must make the decisions (adjudications). The major areas requiring judicial decisions can become very complicated, requiring the judge to make a persistent and critical search for the facts in a case and to balance often-conflicting factors.

Two major issues requiring judicial decisions in guardianship cases are, first, competency and, second, need for guardianship. These are two separate but clearly related issues. If a judge adjudicates a proposed ward to be competent, no need will exist for a guardian to be appointed. If a judge adjudicates a proposed ward to be incompetent (fully or partially is another decision), then the judge must decide if a guardian is needed. An adjudication of incompetency does not mandate appointment of a guardian because, as will be illustrated, other factors must be considered by the judge in reaching a decision about the necessity of appointing a guardian. It may not be in the best interest of a proposed ward, even though found incompetent, to have a guardian appointed. A less restrictive alternative, such as power of attorney, might better serve the proposed ward. If the decision is to appoint a guardian, the sometimes complicated subsequent decision is who to appoint.

Judges' decisions in guardianship cases are based on the state guardianship statute, evidence presented, and consideration of other factors, In many cases, decisions are not difficult, but, as will be illustrated, judicial decisions in guardianship cases can be very complicated and difficult.

In what follows, the matters discussed are evidence, best interest, limited guardianship, and selecting the guardian. Guardianship laws differ among the states, but many principles are common. Although the laws of Georgia will be illustrated, the underlying principles can be extrapolated to the laws of other states.

EVIDENCE

The judge must deal with the standard of proof necessary to find that someone needs a guardian of the person, the property, or both. The most common standard is "clear and convincing evidence." Unfortunately, that standard has no precise definition and is generally defined as falling somewhere between "a preponderance of the evidence" (the standard generally applicable to civil cases) and "beyond a reasonable doubt" (the standard applicable to criminal cases). Since there is no precise definition, the same evidence presented to two different judges may produce two different results because the judges' perception of what constitutes "clear and convincing evidence" differs. In a perfect world, the same evidence would produce the same results, but law has never been an exact science and whether a decision is made by a trained professional (a judge) or by lay people using their collective common reasoning (a jury), the results based on seemingly similar facts can differ. Witnesses should submit all the evidence they believe to be relevant to the issue of competency and the need for guardianship,

Evidence from Professional Evaluators

Under Georgia law, the court must appoint a professional evaluator, designated in the law as a physician or psychologist, to conduct an independent evaluation of the proposed ward and to submit a written Evaluation Report to the court. The Evaluation Report contains a conclusion as to the need for a guardian to be appointed based upon the criteria established by Georgia law. The physician or psychologist is required to state the facts on which the conclusion is based, but the court makes the final decision. The Evaluation Report from the court-appointed physician or psychologist constitutes an independent source of information for the court. This information is apart from any other information about the proposed ward that is provided by physicians, psychologists, clinical social workers, or other professional evaluators who are privately retained by petitioners or by proposed wards to testify on their behalf in cases.

It seems that the law sometimes places an undue burden on the court-appointed professional evaluator, especially when dealing with guardianship of the property of a proposed ward. Physicians or psychologists can make assessments of a person's ability to reason and make decisions concerning their person, but for them to make a determination that a guardian of the estate is needed requires them to have additional information. The physician or psychologist would have to have facts concerning the amount of the proposed ward's assets and how such assets were being managed or mismanaged, and by whom, before drawing a conclusion that a guardian of the estate is or is not necessary.

Court-appointed physicians or psychologists or privately retained professional evaluators who base their determinations of need for a guardian solely on their professional evaluations of proposed wards and who are then called as witnesses in court when the issue of competency is being adjudicated sometimes find themselves on the defensive because they failed to obtain information that might have shown that the proposed ward, even though incompetent, would not need a guardian. It is helpful to the judge and it saves the credibility of the professional evaluator if he or she would acknowledge that if other information had been provided a different conclusion might have been reached. Usually the professional evaluator will then be given some facts and asked whether or not he or she had been made aware of those facts, and if he or she had not been made aware, would this new knowledge change his or her conclusion concerning the need for a guardianship. The professional evaluator should carefully consider the proffered facts and state whether those new facts would cause him or her to reconsider the conclusion.

The professional evaluator is not absolutely required to make a final conclusory statement about the need for guardianship when testifying in person at trial. The professional evaluator should give the judge the benefit of his or her expertise openly and without any bias. There are times when the proposed ward has been a patient of a physician, for example, over a long period of time, and the physician may have a decided opinion about the need for guardianship based on the relationship. Even then, the physician will be subject to questioning in court concerning recent contacts with the proposed ward and other current circumstances of the proposed ward. The physician should answer the questions and offer explanations of how facts that were previously unknown by him or her support the expressed opinion, cause a reassessment of the opinion, or have no bearing on the opinion.

In Georgia, it is possible to have an emergency guardian of the person or the property, or both, appointed (see Emergency Guardianship in chapter 5) prior to a court hearing on the need for the appointment of an emergency guardian if, and only if, a physician or psychologist for the petitioner certifies that "any delay" in the appointment of an emergency guardian is "unreasonable." This requirement seems appropriate if the physician or psychologist is considering a life or death situation or other medical emergency concerning the person of a proposed ward, but the requirement places an undue burden upon a physician or psychologist when it concerns the property of a proposed ward. The physician or psychologist would somehow have to obtain enough reliable data to certify that irreparable waste will occur to the estate of the proposed ward unless an emergency guardian is appointed immediately. This certification is necessary because the court cannot appoint an emergency guardian, pending the hearing on a petition for appointment of an emergency guardian, without the certification of the physician or psychologist.

Georgia law provides that the court may dismiss a petition for guardianship if a court-appointed physician or psychologist finds that the proposed ward does not need a guardian. If the physician or psychologist unequivocally states in the Evaluation Report filed with the court that the proposed ward does not meet the criteria for appointment of a guardian, the court may summarily dismiss the case no matter what the allegations of the petitioner are about the need for a guardian. If the petition for guardianship contained an affidavit completed by a physician or psychologist at the request of the petitioner that stated that the proposed ward needed a guardian, however, the court should refrain from dismissing the petition due to the conflicting reports of the physicians or psychologists. The court must review the Evaluation Report and determine whether to dismiss the petition or to schedule a hearing on the issue of the need for a guardian. Dismissing a petition for guardianship of the person based on an assessment by a court-appointed physician or psychologist is easier than dismissing a petition for guardianship of the property because the physician or psychologist can base his or her conclusion about the need for guardianship of the person solely on an evaluation of the proposed ward. The physician or psychologist can usually determine whether the proposed ward has sufficient understanding or capacity to make significant responsible decisions concerning his or her own person (see chapter 3).

If the proposed ward is capable of making decisions, it does not matter whether the decisions are good or bad. For example, adult children of a proposed ward may feel a guardian is necessary because their elderly father is writing checks to a young woman. However, the physician or psychologist appointed by the court may determine that the elderly father is aware of his circumstances and is making rational, albeit foolish, decisions. The court may dismiss a petition based on such information contained in the Evaluation Report filed by the court-appointed professional evaluator because a rational person is allowed to make foolish decisions. If a guardianship was established for every person who made a bad decision concerning his or her own property, there would be few people who did not have a guardian and those few would be overburdened serving as guardian for numerous other people. Stupidity is not grounds for the appointment of a guardian.

Conflicting Professional Opinions

Judges must contend with competing professional evaluators. Two physicians or two psychologists may conduct separate evaluations of the same person and arrive at opposite conclusions concerning the need for guardianship. One of the most difficult tasks for a judge is to decide which conclusion is to be accepted as being correct. It is a rare instance when one professional evaluator's credentials, analysis, and evidence are so much better than another's that a judge's decision as to which one is correct is easily made. When one of the competing conclusions does not clearly outweigh the other, the judge must use some other parameters in deciding which is correct.

One deciding factor used by judges is familiarity with a physician or psychologist witness. If one physician or psychologist has testified before the judge in other cases, the judge will ordinarily give weight to past history, particularly if the professional evaluator's opinion has been proven to be almost always correct. Being wrong on more than one occasion in the past may lessen a professional evaluator's credibility, but not to the same extent that being correct heightens credibility.

All the Evidence—A Case

Sometimes the evidence produced at trial presents a different picture than that shown by the pleadings and the court-appointed physician's or psychologist's evaluation. For example, there was a case in which two adult children petitioned for guardianship of their mother because she had sold real property and personally financed the sale on terms over a period of years without receiving a deed to secure the debt on the property sold. A deed to secure debt allows for easy foreclosure of the real property sold and financed if the payments go into default. The proposed ward became angry and refused to cooperate during the court-ordered evaluation by a professional evaluator. The professional evaluator appointed by the court relied on the information provided by the children and concluded that a guardian of the property was necessary.

At trial, evidence was introduced that the proposed ward could not read or write, that she had inherited considerable real estate holdings from the estate of her late husband, and that she had recently sold real property without obtaining a deed to secure debt. The proposed ward took the stand in her own behalf and testified that she did not believe that being unable to read or write meant that she needed a guardian. She said that she had not been able to read or write for her entire lifetime and had never been taken advantage of because of that inability. She admitted that she did not receive a deed to secure debt on the real property transaction of which her children were complaining, but she stated that, if it were such a big deal and if everyone thought it was so important, she would get a deed to secure debt in the future as she sold others of her holdings. She testified that she did not know why this had become such an issue because she had sold and financed many parcels of real property in the past without ever taking a deed to secure debt. She had never lost one penny on any of her transactions because she always dealt with people whom she judged to be honest and trustworthy, and they always turned out to be just that. The petitioners could not refute any of the mother's testimony.

The mother ended her testimony by stating that her daughters had really filed the petition for guardianship because she was about to give a prime piece of real property to her son. Her daughters hated her son and did not want him to receive the gift, but she thought it fair since she had already given both of her daughters real property without anyone questioning her competency. This case is a prime example of how a case for guardianship can look convincing on paper, but the judge must reserve judgment until that last bit of evidence is introduced.

WARD'S BEST INTERESTS

The ultimate decision of whether or not a guardian should be appointed often falls outside the parameters of strict medical and legal definitions of competency or incompetency. Georgia law has a provision that no guardian should be appointed for a proposed ward unless the appointment is in the best interests of the proposed ward. A proposed ward might meet the strict legal criteria to have a guardian appointed, but because of outside factors a judge may decide against appointing a guardian.

Power of Attorney—An Example

A person might be incompetent to manage funds or make decisions concerning any financial matters, and the property of the person could be at great risk. All the facts might support the immediate appointment of a guardian of the property. Yet the person might also have previously executed a power of attorney (see chapter 1) for financial affairs. Generally, the appointment of a guardian will cause the revocation of a power of attorney by operation of law. The court must be made aware of the existence of a valid power of attorney, that is, one that was properly executed under the terms of the law in effect where the document was signed and that has not been subsequently revoked by the principal. The court will want to determine if a power of attorney, considered as an alternative to guardianship, is accomplishing all of the goals that a guardianship of the property would accomplish. In such an instance, guardianship would not be in the best interests of the person.

There are times, however, when it is the existence of the power of attorney that precipitates the filing of the petition for guardianship. At such times, the agent is the one who is dissipating the principal's estate for the personal gain of the agent. There are other times when the power of attorney does not accomplish the goals intended. For instance, the power may be poorly drafted and leave out some necessary powers or it may be too vague as to intent. Some financial institutions may refuse to honor the power of attorney for one of these reasons or because the institution fears that the principal lacked legal capacity when the document was executed or that the power has been revoked by some act. The agent may find guardianship more feasible than an action to enforce the power of attorney.

Parens Patriae—Another Example

There are times when social service caseworkers, physicians, or psychologists will invoke the *parens patriae* philosophy of guardianship (see chapter 2). These are times when they believe a person is acting in a manner not in his or her best interests and, therefore, the state should use its sovereign power to protect a person from himself or herself. A case in point involved a woman who had a lump in her breast that her physician believed to be cancer. The woman refused to allow a biopsy that would prove whether or not she had a malignant tumor. The appropriate state social service agency was contacted to investigate. After the woman refused to allow a biopsy even at the urging of the caseworker, the caseworker and the physician joined in a petition for the appointment of a guardian who could authorize the biopsy even against the woman's wishes. Their premise was that the woman could not make a rational, informed decision concerning her own health because a competent person would seek immediate treatment. They relied heavily on the fact that the woman had told them she did not have cancer. They felt that such denial was proof that the woman was not making a rational decision. The court-appointed professional evaluator agreed with the caseworker and the physician that guardianship was necessary because he concluded that the woman was not cognizant of her medical condition and the likely consequences of her inaction.

At trial, the women testified in a very cogent manner that she was not denying that she might have cancer. She said she had decided that, even if a biopsy proved that she had a malignant tumor, she would not seek treatment. She had been informed that the only treatment, if she did indeed have a malignant tumor, was a radical mastectomy of both breasts. She testified that at her age (she was in her late 70s) she did not deem such radical surgery as the best option for her since she felt that her days were numbered and that she would rather live out her life with her breasts intact even if her life were somewhat shortened. She did not deny that she had told the case-worker that she did not have cancer, but she said that she only did so after no one would listen when she tried to explain that she would not have radical surgery at her age. She said that when she began denying that she had cancer, people finally stopped arguing with her about the surgery. She clearly understood the consequences of her actions and was making an informed choice. Guardianship intervention not only was inappropriate in her case but also would have been an egregious invasion of her privacy.

LIMITED GUARDIANSHIP

There is a trend toward more individually customized guardianships. Parry and Hurme (1991) reported that in 1980, the American Bar Association recommended that states enact laws allowing appointment of limited or partial guardians. They added that "when this resolution was adopted, very few states included explicit provisions allowing limited guardianships. Forty-two states now have such legislation. . . ." (p. 304). The push for limited guardianships continued with the recommendation by the Commission on National Probate Court Standards (1993) that courts always consider using limited guardianships: "If the court determines that a guardianship is necessary, the respondent's self-reliance, autonomy, and independence should be promoted by restricting the authority of the guardian to the minimum required for the situation, rather than routinely granting full powers of guardianship in every case" (p. 67).

Under Georgia law, the appointment of a guardian of the person for an individual removes from that individual the power to contract marriage, to make other contracts, to consent to medical treatment, to establish a residence or place of abode, and to bring or defend any action at law or equity personally (except an action relating to the guardianship itself). The appointment of a guardian of the property removes the power to bring any action at law or equity (except an action relating to the guardianship); to make contracts; to buy, sell, or otherwise dispose of or encumber real, personal or trust property; and to enter into other business or commercial transactions. The Georgia law provides that the judge may allow the ward to retain any of the powers just mentioned, however. Appointment of a guardian does not automatically remove the power of a ward to make a will or to vote. Both of those powers must be independently determined according to the law.

Limited guardianships can create problems for people who deal with the guardian or with the ward. Under a general guardianship without limitation, a person dealing with the guardian can require that the guardian produce his or her "Letters of Guardianship" (the official court document issued to a guardian showing the guardian's authority to act for the ward) before accepting the guardian's authority to bind the ward's person or estate. As an extra precaution, some people require the guardian to provide a copy of the Letters of Guardianship with the issuing court's certification that the letters are still in full force and effect. If the guardianship is limited in any degree, the order of the court appointing the guardian will reflect the limitation, but, unless the Letters of Guardianship incorporate by reference the limitation cited in the order, a person dealing with the guardian may be unaware of the limitation. Most people who deal with guardians are unaccustomed to reading the Letters of Guardianship because they expect all of them to be the same. Only if the Letters of Guardianship appear to be customized will they be read carefully.

The negative aspect of limited guardianships could be that fewer people would willingly deal with a guardian whose powers were limited because they would not want to be burdened with having to read and interpret possibly long court documents to determine whether the guardian has the authority to bind the person or the estate of the ward. The ward who retains certain rights might also find fewer people willing to deal with him or her if people have trouble understanding the ward's retention of powers or if there is any question as what exact powers the ward retains. It may be simpler for the person with whom the ward wishes to deal to decline any transaction with the ward. The positive aspect of limited guardianship is that it allows the ward to retain some absolute control over specified aspects of his or her life, thus allowing the ward to retain some self-reliance, autonomy, and independence.

A Case In Point

A limited guardianship can be established for a specific purpose, and its existence will not be widely known even though it is a matter of public record. A case in point concerned an older woman who borrowed $10,000.00 from a financial institution when she purchased her home. When the woman had paid the financial institution exactly $10,000.00, she refused to make any further payments. She seemed oblivious to the concept of interest on this loan. The financial institution, as mortgage holder, did not want to foreclose on the woman's home. The woman's employer and the woman's daughter tried to work out an arrangement whereby the employer would withhold a part of the woman's pay and the daughter would make payment to the mortgage holder. The woman refused to authorize any such plan and demanded all of her pay.

The daughter petitioned for guardianship of the estate. At trial, the evidence showed that the woman was in excellent mental and physical health and had worked for the same employer for many years. The employer testified that she was reliable and competent, and she had no trouble handling money or paying any of her debts except for the mortgage. The woman testified that she did not owe any more money on her home because she knew she borrowed $10,000.00, kept accurate records, and knew she had repaid $10,000.00. It was interesting to note that the woman regularly used a department store charge card and had no problem comprehending the principle of interest as applied to the charge card. Yet she could not be convinced that the same principle applied to her mortgage.

This was a perfect case for a limited guardianship. The guardian was authorized by the court to receive from the employer the exact amount of the monthly mortgage payment as the payment became due and to make the payment to the mortgage holder. The guardian had no other power. The woman insisted that she did not owe any more on her home, but she acquiesced to the limited guardianship. Except that the establishment of the limited guardianship was a public record, the only people outside of the court who were informed of the creation of the limited guardianship were the woman, her daughter who was appointed as limited guardian, her employer, and the mortgage holder. The woman remained in complete control of her life, and the only effect of the limited guardianship on her personally was the loss of personal control of money in the amount of the monthly mortgage payment. The woman retained her home, the mortgage was paid, and, importantly, the woman never had to admit that she was wrong because she never had to make another mortgage payment personally.

Choice of Abode

The most commonplace use of a limited guardianship is allowing a ward to choose a place of abode. Some proposed wards realize that they can no longer make appropriate decisions concerning their persons, but they have such a fear of being placed in a nursing home that they fight a guardianship they may otherwise welcome. Some elderly people attribute loss of mental acuity to the pressure of the responsibilities that they have endured since adulthood and actually welcome guardianship as a relief from those responsibilities.

Some potential guardians will testify that they have no plans to place a ward in a nursing home, but the proposed ward may still be skeptical. Other potential guardians may want to place a ward in a nursing home simply because it would be easier on them. If a judge sees a case in which a guardianship is necessary, but the judge deems that the guardianship would be more palatable to the ward if the ward retained the power to choose a place of abode, then the judge should allow the ward that power. It is necessary, of course, that the ward have the resources to maintain the place of abode and retain sufficient ADL skills to make living there feasible. Most modern guardianship laws require that the guardianship be the least restrictive possible, and the judge should be attuned to this consideration even if the parties involved do not address the possibilities on their own.

SELECTING THE GUARDIAN

Most contested guardianship cases do not involve the issue of whether or not a guardianship should be established but, rather, who should be guardian. In Georgia, there are enumerated classes of people who must be considered for appointment as guardian in priority order, and a person can be passed over only for good cause shown. The first preference is a person nominated in writing by the proposed ward while he or she was competent. The spouse of the proposed ward is next entitled and is followed by an adult child of the proposed ward. Other persons, including other relatives, are then listed, culminating in the appointment of the director of the county department of family and children services as guardian of the person and the county guardian as guardian of the property when there are no other suitable persons available to appoint.

In cases where there are competing nominated guardians, it is rare that one is acting solely in the best interests of the ward and the other is acting solely for self-interest. It is rarer still to find two competing nominated guardians who are both acting solely in the best interests of the proposed ward. It is common to have the competing nominated guardians both acting solely in their own self-interest, but the most common contested case involves competing nominated guardians who are acting in a combination of best interests of the ward and self-interest.

A judge's decision in a case may turn on such a factor as the plans the competing nominated guardians have for the ward's care. The judge must evaluate the prospective plans and determine which would be of greater overall benefit to the ward. The judge must analyze (1) the obvious benefits of the plan to the ward; (2) whether the plan also benefits the nominee proposing the plan and, if so, whether the benefit to the nominee is greater than the benefit to the ward; and (3) whether the plan of the nominee is detrimental to the interests of the other nominee and, if so, whether the benefit derived by the ward outweighs the detriment to the other nominee. In this analysis, the judge must sometimes discern the motives of the nominees.

For instance, a common occurrence involves one nominee proposing to place the ward in a nursing home and the other nominee proposing to keep the ward at home. All things being equal, the judge would likely favor the nominee who proposes to keep the ward at home because most people would prefer to be at home. The person who proposes to place the ward in a nursing home, however, may have made the decision because the ward cannot receive the necessary care at home, the ward cannot afford to pay for the necessary care at home, or the ward's assets would be depleted too quickly if home care was provided, thereby causing the ward to become destitute when placement in a nursing home would have allowed the ward to live within the ward's means for the remainder of the ward's life. The judge must also consider the possibility that the nominee wants to place the ward in a nursing home to save money that the nominee will inherit after the death of the ward. The judge must weigh the interests of the ward against the interests of the nominee.

The nominee who wants to keep the ward at home may have made the decision because the ward can receive adequate care at home, the ward can afford any extra cost occasioned by living at home, or the ward's assets are such that the ward could remain at home for some period of time before conservation of assets becomes a major factor in considering more restrictive placement for the ward, or a combination of these. The judge must also consider whether the nominee is likely to spend unwisely in order to unnecessarily deplete the estate so that another person will inherit little upon the ward's death. The judge must decide in the ward's interest, and any residual benefit to another person is collateral.

The judge, as the trier of fact, must follow general rules of evidence to try to reconcile conflicting evidence so that it speaks the truth. In a contest between competing nominees, however, the judge often must discern the motives behind the facts. No nominee may be perfect, or even desirable, and each may offer positive and negative features to consider. Sometimes the judge must choose the lesser of two evils when selecting a guardian. If one of two equally qualified nominees has a preference conferred by statute, the choice is easy. If the nominees stand on equal footing both legally and factually, the judge must make a Solomonic decision. The quality of life of the ward may depend on the person selected by the judge.

Competing Nominees—Son versus Daughter

Consider the case in which the only daughter, a resident of Georgia, filed for guardianship of her father, a resident of Florida, and the only son, a resident of Tennessee, filed an objection to the daughter's appointment.

Some background to this case is necessary. The son had told the daughter that he was fearful for their father living alone after their mother's death and that he was considering moving the father into a nursing home near his home. The daughter immediately brought the father home with her. She thought it would be unfair for the father to live near her brother because her brother had a wife and children living at home whereas she was divorced and her children had all left home. She, therefore, thought she should have the father with her.

The father had executed a power of attorney naming his son as agent before his daughter took him to her home. The son considered that it would be more appropriate to sell the home place rather than trying to rent it since no family member lived near the property. When the son sold the property, he placed the proceeds from the sale in a bank account in the joint names of the father and the son, with a right of survivorship. The father had another bank account that would be equally divided between the son and the daughter after the father's death. When the daughter discovered that the son had established the joint account with right of survivorship from the proceeds of the sale of the home, she filed for guardianship.

The evidence adduced at trial included the fact that the father's will provided that the son inherit the home place after the father's death because it was the father's intent to equalize a lifetime of gifts made to the daughter by both the father and the mother. After the daughter's divorce, her parents

bailed her out of tight financial situations and paid for the college education of each of her children at her insistence. The son thought that the establishment of the joint account with right of survivorship from the
proceeds of the sale of the home place would ensure that his father's wishes
were carried out.

Unfortunately for the son, the will of the father did not provide that the
son would have any interest in the proceeds from a sale of the home place
if the home place was sold in the father's lifetime. The son thought he acted
appropriately in establishing the joint account because his father's intent
was to equalize the distributions made to both children, and the establishment of the joint account would carry out the father's intent. The daughter
admitted that her parents had given more to her than to her brother, but she
also pointed out that the parents had been very generous to her brother as
well. She testified that since her brother had begun acting as agent for the
father under the power of attorney, the brother continued to give money to
the daughter as she requested it, but he now always gave himself an equal
amount. The daughter did not approve of her brother getting an equal
amount of money because, in her opinion, her brother did not need it as
much as she did. The son did not object to his sister's continuing to receive
money so long as he received an equal amount.

The father needed a guardian to protect his assets from his own children.
Guardianship would protect the father's assets because the guardian, whoever it was, could not make future gifts or loans to the children without
prior court approval.

The son admitted that his father was receiving excellent care in the
daughter's home, but he thought the father would benefit if moved to a
nursing home near the son's home because more family members (i.e., the
son's wife and children) could visit him if he were closer to the son's
home. The son also thought that the daughter's past financial history and
her reliance on her parent's money should preclude her serving as guardian
of the father's property. The daughter admitted that her brother would be
a better choice to serve as guardian of the property, provided that she was
allowed to serve as guardian of the person and was reasonably compen-
sated for her services in providing full-time care for her father.

Since the father was receiving excellent care in his daughter's home, the
court determined that it would not be in the father's interest to bring in
strangers to serve as guardians provided that the assets were protected and
secured by proper bond. The court offered to appoint the daughter as
guardian of the person and the son as guardian of the property if the daugh-

ter and son could agree on a reasonable compensation for the daughter for her care of the father and if the son would consent to using the funds held in the joint account first if it became necessary to encroach upon the corpus of the father's estate. The son and daughter reached an agreement and were appointed as co-guardians. The father's interests were protected from abuse by his children, he was allowed to live with his daughter, and his son continued to handle the father's financial affairs under court scrutiny.

SUMMARY

The judge in a guardianship case can be faced with some very perplexing problems. What is fact in the face of conflicting information from professional evaluators? Is a guardianship in the best interests of the respondent? What powers should be retained for the ward in a limited guardianship? Who should be the guardian in a contested case? The judge decides.

REFERENCES

Commission on National Probate Court Standards (1993). *National Probate Court Standards*. Williamsburg, VA: National Center for State Courts.
Parry, J. W. & Hurme, S. B. (1991). Guardianship monitoring and enforcement nationwide. *Mental and Physical Disability Law Reporter, 15*(3), 304–314.

CHAPTER 8

Guardianship and Abuse of Dependent Adults

Isabella Horton Grant and Mary Joy Quinn

Over the past two decades, abuse of adults has received increasing public attention. The 1970s saw the emergence of the battered woman syndrome. In 1978, testimony was given to Congress by Dr. Suzanne Steinmetz, a national authority in the field of family violence, who called specific attention to the abuse and neglect of the elderly. Physical and sexual abuse of younger adults who are developmentally disabled is now well documented. Studies have documented financial and psychological abuse and neglect of dependent adults (Pillemer & Finkelhor, 1988; Podnieks, 1992) as well as violations of their due process and other constitutional rights (U.S. House of Representatives, 1981; Wolf & Pillemer, 1984; Wolf & Pillemer, 1989).

Following a nationwide study by the AP (1987), concern about abuse and neglect of impaired adults led Congress (U.S. House of Representatives, 1988) to focus on guardianships. The AP study uncovered widespread abuse of wards and misuse of the guardianship process. There was considerable evidence of lack of due process in court proceedings, dissipation of estates through inadequate court monitoring, and unnecessary global removal of rights. It was also shown that many courts lacked or disregarded important information from medical and social service agencies having special knowledge of the elderly and dependent adult populations. Concerns were also raised with respect to the function and role of individual guardians, with many cited instances of abuse and neglect and lack of judicial remedies or concerns.

In the wake of the Associated Press report, legislatures, courts, and individual judges took steps to reform the guardianship process (see the Wingspread Conference in chapter 10). The concept of the least restrictive alternative was developed in order to put major emphasis on the best interest of proposed wards. This concept was applied both to living situations and to legal methods for the care of property and finances of persons unable to manage for themselves. As explained in the section on limited guardianship in the previous chapter, legislatures and individual courts created ways to tailor guardianships to individual situations so that wards did not lose rights unnecessarily and so independence could be maximized. In many states, court visitors, court investigators, or *guardians ad litem* were designated to visit proposed wards, advise them of rights, and examine the particular circumstances of each case (see chapters 5 and 9). Recommendations for court action could then be made on the basis of more complete information.

Guardianship petitions, when they pertain to adults, are most commonly filed on behalf of the elderly, but they are also filed for other groups of adults, i.e., those who are developmentally disabled, mentally ill, or the victims of a catastrophic illness or accident. These are the people who are vulnerable and partially or totally dependent on others to handle their personal and financial affairs. The great bulk of institutions and individuals who are appointed as guardians are not abusive or neglectful in any manner. In fact, some can be safely labeled heroic in the care and attention given to their wards. Abuse and neglect of dependent adults is a fact in too many instances, however. In 1991, Congress estimated that 5% of the elderly every year are abused or neglected. In order to understand the problem better, it is necessary to examine the types of abuse and neglect as well as some of their signs and symptoms.

ABUSE AND NEGLECT

Physical Abuse

In general, physical abuse means that an individual has been physically harmed either by others or by self. The causes of physical harm could be assault, medication mismanagement, lack of medical care or improper medical care. A variety of injuries from abuse may occur, including burns from cigarettes or ropes (from being restrained), abrasions, bruises, fractures, dislocations, welts, wounds, rashes, sores, internal injuries, genital or urinary irritation, presence of sexually transmitted disease, head trauma, and punctures. There may be unusual findings from blood and urine testing that could indicate dehydration or lack of proper nutrition. Some injuries may be difficult to understand or accept. In one highly publicized case, a 61-year old-university teacher assaulted her 86- year-old mother in the family home and inflicted more than 20 bites. The mother survived the attack but only after extensive medical treatment, skin grafting, and physical therapy. She deteriorated physically and mentally and had to be placed in a nursing home so that her daily needs could be met. The daughter had no memory of the attack; it had happened while she was intoxicated. The mother remembered the attack and declined to have her daughter visit her in the nursing home because she was too afraid of her. To the outside world, the daughter appeared to be devoted and only interested in her mother's welfare. She was, however, a remarkably angry woman who was very authoritarian. The Public Guardian petitioned to be the guardian. The daughter was interviewed by a court investigator. At that time, the daughter was incarcerated as a result of the attack. She objected to the Public Guardian being appointed and felt she should be appointed guardian.

It is not always easy to determine whether abuse has occurred. The usual explanation given for bruises and injuries is to say that the person fell. Both victims and suspected abusers will give this explanation. In fact, in the case just referred to, the mother initially told emergency room personnel that she had fallen and that was how she had sustained all her injuries. She later acknowledged that she had been attacked by her daughter. It can be determined whether injuries are due to abuse by paying attention to clinical signs and descriptions of the "incident" (Quinn & Tomita, 1986). For instance, if there are bruises at different stages of healing all over the body, the explanation that the person fell the day before is implausible. This is particularly true if the bruises are bilateral and resemble hand or object prints. Suspicions should also be aroused if the care giver and the victim give conflicting accounts of the "fall." There may be "doctor hopping" or abandonment of a vulnerable adult in an emergency room. A full medical evaluation including a neuropsychological examination may be necessary to determine whether abuse in fact took place.

Neglect

Most states have mandatory reporting laws with regard to abuse and neglect of vulnerable adults. Typically the highest number of cases reported are those of neglect, and they are commonly linked with financial abuse. The neglect may be active, which means that the necessities of life such as food, water, clothing, shelter, and medication are deliberately withheld by the person the vulnerable person depends on. Passive neglect means that the necessities of life are being withheld through the ignorance or the incapacity of the care giver. Both neglect and abuse can result in serious permanent injury or death.

The most common scenario in neglect is the failure to thrive Syndrome. The symptoms may include malnutrition, dehydration, abnormal blood chemistry values such as excess blood sodium due to dehydration, and excess blood sugar because insulin is not properly administered. There may also be pressure sores or deprivational behaviors such as clinging, taking up the time of authorities or outsiders, gobbling food, excess thirst, and dulled expression. Neglect can occur in situations where there is alcohol abuse, dementia, depression, including bereavement, and where caregiving systems have broken down or the individual refuses assistance. In one situation, two elderly sisters slowly starved to death in a board and care home after their nephew divorced their care giver and left the home. The care giver had given good care for a number of years, but after the divorce she stopped tending to the two women and left them in their own excrement. Both later died from malnutrition and dehydration.

Psychological Abuse

Psychological abuse is characterized by the mental suffering of the victim. It can include harassment and manipulation, name calling, threats (particularly of abandonment and placement in a nursing home), and withholding of critical information. Manifestations in the victim of this type of abuse are expressions of shame, confusion, fearfulness and trembling, and cowering in the presence of the care giver. Caution must be taken in defining a situation as psychologically abusive because some families have always yelled at each other, and yelling may be the "family style." Also, some behaviors are common to chronic diseases associated with aging such as trembling with Parkinsonism and confusion with the various dementias. Psychological abuse is most likely present when there are other types of abuse and neglect.

Undue influence is properly discussed under psychological abuse. Undue influence is the substitution of one person's will for the true desires of another. It can be accompanied by fraud, duress, or different types of pressure on persons who are particularly susceptible, such as incapacitated elderly. Examples are found all too often in the probate court and involve elderly men and women who have been isolated from their families by new found "friends" and are alleged to have made gifts of their own free will (see chapter 1). When past bank accounts are examined or relatives and old friends are consulted, however, it is clear that these "gifts" are quite out of the ordinary for the victim. One woman who watched her pennies all her life suddenly depleted her savings account by giving extensive gifts such as cars and boats to her neighbors, something that was not at all in character for her. Another all too common occurrence is the "housekeeper syndrome," involving a designing person employed to assist a dependent adult who then isolates the adult by telling family and friends to call before coming to visit. When family and friends do call, the housekeeper tells them that "Aunt Lillian is resting" and cannot come to the phone or that "Aunt Lillian is not feeling up to a visitor." Gradually the dependent adult comes to feel that the only friend she has is the housekeeper. The housekeeper or new found "friend" reinforces that belief by telling Aunt Lillian that no one is calling but that he or she will always be there to take care of her. Frequently, a new will is drawn up at that point and all assets are left to the housekeeper or friend. Durable powers of attorney and revocable trusts are also often found in these situations, and in many instances they are prepared by an attorney engaged by the friend.

Financial Abuse

Financial abuse is extremely common, particularly with the elderly who have assets. In fact, any impaired adult who has assets, regardless of the source (personal injury lawsuit, earned income, or inheritance), is at risk for financial abuse. Financial abuse means that assets are being misappropriated, usually through force or through misrepresentation of facts to a person who has partial or complete incapacity. One study of conservatorship court cases found that two thirds of all elder abuse cases were financial abuse (Jones, 1990). In one case that came to the court's attention, an elderly woman was taken advantage of by a younger woman who came to the house selling door to door. Within a year, the saleswoman had moved the elderly woman out of her own home into a house that was purchased for cash using only the elderly woman's money that had been put in their joint names. The younger woman moved into the house along with other members of her family. At the same time, the younger woman was charging exorbitant prices for in-home care and isolating the elderly woman from caring relatives. A new will gave all the assets to the younger woman, including complete ownership of the new property. The situation was resolved only after an independent guardian was appointed by the court and all assets were taken out of the control of the younger woman.

In still another financial abuse case, an elderly woman was taken advantage of by a longtime friend who held her power of attorney. When a relative suspected that the friend was financially abusing his power, she petitioned the court to have a guardianship established. The facts were egregious enough for a temporary or emergency guardianship to be established immediately (see chapter 5). When the temporary guardian was appointed, the court also ordered that financial accounting be made by the friend. After the temporary guardianship was in place, however, the friend took the elderly woman to Reno, Nevada, and married her. She did not have the capacity to know that she was getting married, and later the marriage was annulled by the court. A review of the financial records indicated that a great deal of the woman's money had been squandered and that numerous parcels of real property had been sold below market value. The longtime friend and his friends had the run of the elderly woman's mansion while she had been relegated to servant quarters in the basement.

Indicators of financial abuse may include

- tardiness in paying bills or lack of payment at all,
- absence of visible means of support on the part of the guardian or care giver,
- unusual interest in the amount of money spent on the person's care,
- concern that too much money is being spent,
- unusual activity in a bank account such as frequent ATM withdrawals when the person cannot walk or "churning" bank accounts,
- sudden withdrawals from bank accounts when the person is brought to the bank by a "new friend,"
- disconnected utilities,

- missing property,
- exorbitant charges for personal services, and
- failure to meet deadlines for court accountings.

Violation of Rights

All Americans have certain inalienable rights as determined by the Constitution, statutes, and case law. A concern in the field of guardianship is the lack of due process in the establishment of guardianships and in their functioning. Due process includes making sure that a proposed ward is aware of and understands to the best of his or her ability the implications of a guardianship. Further, the proposed ward should have his or her rights explained by a neutral party. A proposed ward has many rights, for example, the right to have an attorney, to request a jury trial, and to ask that someone other than the proposed guardian serve as the guardian. The person giving information about rights should not be a party to the action, should know the law, and should be experienced in methods of communicating with impaired adults.

Violations of rights by guardians include failure to provide spending money, not sustaining the ward in the manner to which he or she is accustomed, and placing the ward in a setting that is more restrictive than necessary. Other violations of wards' rights include not permitting them to vote, to practice their religion, to open their mail, or to receive visitors. Wards have the right to be treated with dignity, to have friends, to be properly cared for and not neglected, and to lead their lives in the least restrictive manner possible consistent with their abilities.

ABUSE BY PETITIONERS

Petitions for guardianships are filed for a variety of reasons, usually for very pragmatic and protective reasons. Often there is a health crisis, such as a stroke, which has rendered an individual incapable of performing even the most mundane daily tasks such as bathing, grooming, taking care of household chores, or paying the bills. It also happens that third parties such as banks or brokerage houses may refuse to honor powers of attorney. A guardianship petition may be filed because a probate judge recommends it after learning that a beneficiary of a will is incapable of handling an inheritance. Physicians may urge family members to apply when a relative is failing and there are questions about the relative's ability to consent to medical treatment.

The motive for petitioning for guardianship may be benevolent, or there may be an intent to abuse. The petitioner may have mixed motives or may not know what else to do. Many people are not aware of the alternatives to guardianship, or they may particularly desire court supervision for complex estates or a difficult family that is quarreling over the impaired adult's care or money, or both. Sometimes friends and family become desperate as they see a loved one failing and giving unreasonable sums of money to strangers or not paying legitimate bills. At other times, family members become afraid that an elder is spending what they consider to be their inheritance or that other siblings are maneuvering the elder into making a will that favors them. They file for guardianship as a way of gaining control over the situation. In still other instances, family members or friends may suspect that the person holding a power of attorney is being abusive or embezzling funds. As noted in the example earlier in this chapter, appointment of a guardian may be needed to determine whether there is abuse and then to remedy any abusive actions.

When petitions stem from an altruistic motive, there is a genuine desire to benefit another human being. These petitions are often initiated by members of the helping professions as well as by friends and family. The bulk of petitions fall into this category. In one instance, a son petitioned to be named guardian of his 93-year-old father after his father had had three strokes. The son was able to adjust his business affairs so that he could be his father's care giver. He said that it was always understood in his family that ailing family members would be taken care of by other family members.

Occasionally, petitions are filed and it is clear from the outset that the petitioner is abusing the proposed ward, has an intent to abuse, or has a history of being abusive. In one jurisdiction, a daughter who held a durable power of attorney for her ailing mother filed for guardianship. During the process of the investigation, other family members came forward and stated that the daughter had been using her mother's money for herself. The court ordered the daughter to make an accounting of her financial transactions as attorney in fact for her mother. The allegations were sustained; the daughter had been using her mother's money for her own benefit. Filing for guardianship was simply a way for the daughter to gain even more control over her mother's financial affairs and to fend off other concerned family members. The court determined that the daughter should make restitution and appointed a neutral party to serve as guardian.

Some petitions are simply a misuse of the guardianship process. In one case, an elderly woman caused a petition for guardianship to be filed for a neighbor because of a dispute over the volume of a television set. The proposed ward was also elderly, but an investigation determined she did not need a guardianship.

Some petitions are filed when there are mixed motives. The impaired adult may need care, but it appears that the petitioner is more concerned about other matters such as exerting control over family finances to the exclusion of other siblings.

Sometimes a power of attorney or trust has been abused and only a guardianship with its attendant legal powers can serve to remove a wrongdoer from authority or responsibility. A guardian can take steps to recover misappropriated assets and can also file a lawsuit for medical costs and damages resulting from physical abuse, neglect, or financial abuse.

Recent reforms in guardianship law have stressed the importance of the least restrictive legal option when surrogate decision making is indicated. Guardianship, with its attendant court costs and supervision, is viewed as the most restrictive legal option. Less restrictive options exist as alternatives to guardianship, including informal arrangements, powers of attorney, and trusts. In many cases, the less restrictive option may be appropriate. For example, a capable elder may execute a power of attorney for the management of her affairs rather than come under a guardianship of the estate. One must consider, however, that a less restrictive option also means less protection for the elder and less accountability for the person handling the elder's affairs (Overman, 1991). It is certainly more convenient for someone to manage another person's life and money under a power of attorney than to follow strict court requirements for guardianship. In many cases, however, the accountability and protection inherent in guardianships may be preferable. As one attorney noted, "Least restrictive alternative? For whom—the victim or the abuser?" (J. Ferdon, personal communication, March 3, 1992).

ABUSE BY GUARDIANS

Most guardianships function in the best interests of the ward, and some guardians are amazingly creative and heroic in providing opportunities and comfort for their incapacitated wards. A guardian can become abusive at any time during the course of guardianship, however. Sometimes it depends on how stressed they are; at other times, it depends on how greedy they are. In still other instances, guardians may be incapable of handling the money or may become impaired themselves. Some guardians become financially abusive when the ward becomes so frail as to not recognize them any more. Others "borrow" money believing that the impaired person would wish them to have it but then fail to pay it back even though they intend to do so.

Guardians themselves can become impaired and cease functioning. In one instance, a ward in her 80s recognized that her guardian, a family friend, had stopped sending her personal allowance checks, and she realized when he visited that he now had severe memory deficits. Since she had regained capacity, she petitioned for termination of the guardianship, which was granted by the court. In another instance, a husband became the guardian of his wife's estate and then fell under the influence of a bar maid and her husband. He began drinking heavily, stopped paying the nursing home bills, and confessed to being "crazy" about the bar maid. He purchased her fur coats and a boat and eventually went through his wife's entire estate, including the proceeds of the family home that they co-owned. He became destitute and then was abandoned by his new "friends" (see the quotation from Schillingburg in chapter 1).

Some guardians believe it is their duty to conserve the ward's money either because it seems to be the wise thing to do or because they are saving money for the heirs, of which they may be one. In one case, a guardian failed to use for the care of the ward any of the income or principle from a million dollar trust left to a developmentally disabled adult by her mother. The guardian reasoned that the ward's basic care was being provided for by money from public benefits. He further reasoned that he should not use any of the income for the ward's care because the mother stated in the trust that all sources of income other than the trust should be utilized. In fact, the ward was living in nearly abject poverty in a marginal board and care home with barely adequate clothing. When the ward's mother was alive, the two women had lived together in upper middle class circumstances. The court, on learning of the situation, appointed an attorney to represent the ward. Ultimately, the court ruled that all income from the trust should be applied to the care of the ward as she was in need of special training as well as the necessities of life. Following this ruling, the ward was moved to a private home and began living in much the way she had when her mother was alive. She received increased personal attention and several serious medical problems were uncovered and treated.

Courts have also become aware of possible abuse by private professional guardians, who are a relatively new phenomenon in the guardianship arena. Conflicts of interest may arise, recognized or unrecognized, with the professional guardians. For instance, one private guardianship agency started a home care agency under a different name and then referred all its clients who needed home care to that agency. Fees were being paid from the wards' funds to the guardianship agency and to the home care agency, one and the same agency. In another instance, an individual private professional guardian who was a licensed clinical psychotherapist felt justified in prescribing her therapeutic services for her wards. Instead, she should have referred wards to an independent third party to evaluate the need for psychotherapy and, if needed, then arrange for a psychotherapist other than herself. As a result of these kinds of experiences, courts have come to believe that professional guardians should function as case managers rather than as care providers. As a case manager, a guardian is responsible for arranging and supervising the care a ward receives, not for personally delivering the care.

JUDICIAL REMEDIES FOR ABUSE OF WARDS

Courts, legislators, and the general public have become increasingly aware of the need to protect dependent adults from various types of abuse, including abuse by guardians and the court process itself. Proposed wards are receiving more information and help, including the appointment of attorneys to protect their rights. To prevent abuse, investigative and court monitoring systems are encouraged and mandated in many states (see chapter 9). Volunteer programs have been instituted in some courts to aid in the monitoring role (Miler & Hurme, 1991; Twomey, 1994). In some states, the estate of the ward, if possible, pays a fee for each investigation undertaken by the court.

Most states require that guardians file an annual financial accounting with the court. Screening of guardianship records and requirements of proof that records are accurate are important preventive measures. In one jurisdiction, the simple court requirement for the submission of original bank statements with each accounting to confirm balances uncovered a number of guardian defalcations (misuse of funds). Strictly enforcing the deadlines for filing inventories of wards' assets and annual accountings as well as court-sponsored education for guardians that emphasizes the important fiduciary nature of their role are also important. Some states have developed detailed handbooks and videotapes to aid in the education of guardians. Other states, such as Florida, have mandated training for guardians.

In combating abuse by guardians, courts are empowered to remove guardians, to order the return of estate property, and to award damages, including punitive and double damages. Courts can also surcharge guardians if they have mishandled money or dissipated assets. Guardians can act to remedy abuse by suing for the return of estate property from third persons and by suing former guardians for misapplication of funds. Guardians can also have marriages annulled by the courts and can insist on proper living accommodations for wards. Courts can also order that assessments be made as to the functioning of a proposed ward (see chapter 3). For instance, a multidisciplinary geriatric assessment may provide information that would be helpful in determining where a ward should live and what services should be provided.

Traditional legal actions have often proved inadequate to provide remedies for elder abuse. Maine and California recently enacted legislation particularly aimed at financial exploiters. The Improvident Transfer of Title law in Maine creates a presumption of undue influence if a transfer of property takes place for less than full value to a person with whom the dependent adult has a confidential relationship. California's Elder Abuse and Dependent Adult Civil Protection Act breaks new ground by allowing court costs and attorney's fees to successful plaintiffs and post mortem recovery for pain and suffering up to $250,000. The act also gives the Probate Court general jurisdiction to hear and decide all aspects of claims for relief under the act if a guardian has been appointed (Fighting against financial exploitation, 1992).

SUMMARY

All persons have the right to be free from crime and from abuse by family and institutions whether or not they are dependent and frail. The manner and consequences of infringement of these rights are often far different for dependent adults and older adults than they are for the general public because dependent adults may have a more limited ability to protect themselves. Over the past two decades, the abuse of dependent adults has come to the attention of the public and professional communities, including the courts. As a result, state legislatures and various professional communities have taken steps to prevent abuse.

REFERENCES

Associated Press. (1987). *Guardians of the elderly: An ailing system. A special report.*

Fighting against financial exploitation. (1992, November, December). *Elder Law Forum, 4*, 11.

Jones, C. A. (1990). *Abuse of the frail elderly: Social services and legal implications.* Unpublished manuscript, San Francisco State University.

Miler, S. & Hurme, S. B. (1991, October) Guardianship monitoring: An advocate's role. *Clearinghouse Review, 25*(6).

Overman, W. H. (1991). Preventing elder abuse and neglect through advance legal planning. *Journal of Elder Abuse & Neglect, 3*(4), 5–21.

Pillemer, K. A. & Finkelhor, D. (1988). Prevalence of elder abuse: A random sample survey. *Gerontologist, 23*, 51–57.

Podnieks, E. (1992). National survey on abuse of the elderly in Canada. *Journal of Elder Abuse and Neglect, 4*(1–2), 5–57.

Quinn, M. J. & Tomita, S. K. (1986). *Elder abuse and neglect: Causes, diagnoses, and intervention strategies.* New York: Springer.

Twomey, M. (1994, Spring). AARP's national guardianship monitoring program can be a resource for courts. *NASJE News, 9*(1).

U.S. House of Representatives Select Committee on Aging. (1981). *Elder abuse; An examination of a hidden problem, 97th Congress* (Committee Publication No. 97-277). Washington, DC: U.S. Government Printing Office.

U.S. House of Representatives, Subcommittee on Health and Long-Term Care. (1988). *Abuses in guardianships of the elderly and infirm: A national disgrace, 100th Congress,* (Committee Publication No. 100-641). Washington, DC: U.S. Government Printing Office.

Wolf, R. S. & Pillemer, K. A. (1984). *Working with abused elders; Assessment, advocacy, and intervention.* Worchester, MA: University of Massachusetts, Medical Center.

Wolf, R. S. & Pillemer, K. A. (1989). *Helping elderly victims: The reality of elder abuse.* New York: Columbia University Press.

CHAPTER 9

Monitoring of Guardianship

Sally Balch Hurme

PURPOSE OF MONITORING

Monitoring is the process by which the court that established a guardianship determines that the purpose of the guardianship—to protect an incapacitated person—is being fulfilled. The ward, found to be legally vulnerable and stripped of civil rights, must rely on the court for protection. Once the court has assumed the role of protector, it has a continuing legal and moral duty to make certain that the required protection is a reality. As one court has noted, "the court is the guardian; an individual who is given that title is merely an agent or arm of that tribunal in carrying out its sacred responsibility" (Law v. John Hanson Savings & Loan, 1979).

As made clear in the previous chapter, the court cannot assume that the guardian will act in the ward's best interest, scrupulously manage the ward's assets, effectively assess the ward's needs, and diligently obtain all appropriate services.

> Mrs. Thomas was the guardian for her developmentally disabled adult son. She had been a capable caretaker for her son, but over the years both Mrs. Thomas and her son had grown progressively frail. He became bedridden, and she could no longer lift or turn him. He developed serious bedsores, and she was on the verge of exhaustion trying to take care of him in her home.

She realized that she needed help but had been told that it would be five years before she could place her son in a local care facility.

Mr. Peters was appointed guardian for his minor son, Tim, when Tim received a large settlement from an automobile accident. When Mr. Peters started a business a few years later, he borrowed $30,000 from Tim's estate.

Mrs. Joan Jones agreed to be the guardian for her mother who had Alzheimer's disease and required 24-hour supervision. Over time, this arrangement grew to be very difficult for Joan. She began to leave her bedridden mother alone for long periods because she was frustrated with demands on her time her mother's care required (Miler, 1993, p. 82).

BARRIERS TO MONITORING

Unfortunately, not all courts acknowledge their ongoing role to monitor guardianship cases to make sure guardians are serving the best interests of their wards. Divergence can exist between the theory of what monitoring the courts ought to do and the actual monitoring practices in many courts. There is a noticeable "gap between the nobilities of the ideals that we purport to cherish and the deficiencies and the downright meanness of the procedures that we allow to occur" in guardianship cases, including monitoring (Keilitz, 1992, p. 34). Some courts diligently monitor their guardianship cases; others may do little to provide ongoing oversight of the ward's well-being, reviewing the guardianship only if someone formally petitions the court.

A possible cause for a "hands off" policy in many guardianship cases is the philosophy behind the Uniform Probate Code (UPC). The UPC, first drafted in 1975 by the National Conference of Commissioners on Uniform State Laws, was an attempt to provide uniform probate administration by courts among the various states. An underlying premise of the UPC is that the courts should not be involved in the day-to-day administration of a decedent's estate. "The UPC offered new hope for speedy and inexpensive probate of estates in which there was no substantial legal dispute" (Kindregan, 1979, p. 6). The UPC's predominant theory was to make probate more administrative and less adversarial. The court's role is to be "wholly passive until some interested person invokes its power to secure resolution of a matter" (Uniform Probate Code, 1987).

For historical reasons, guardianship was included in the probate code (Averill, 1978), so guardianship traditionally was part of the probate court's jurisdiction. At the time the probate laws were being modernized, the guardianship laws also needed modernization and uniformity. Thus, under the original UPC, the guardian, like the probate administrator, received little supervision until filing the final accounting when the ward died. Further, this minimal court supervision focused on financial concerns with little consideration of how business matters affected the personal circumstances and well-being of the ward (Hurme, 1991).

Although reduced court supervision may have been a welcome reform to probate administration, the circumstances of a guardianship are different. Unlike the administrator of a decedent's estate who primarily pays the decedent's debts and distributes the remainder to heirs or beneficiaries, a guardian is responsible for the well-being of a living person. Rather than the administrator's sterile business of wrapping up the financial affairs of a deceased person, a guardian is responsible for the ward's day-to-day personal affairs, determining where the ward lives, with whom the ward associates, and what medical treatment, education, or rehabilitation the ward receives. This may be an ongoing process for years or even decades for a young adult under guardianship. These far-reaching responsibilities are far more complex socially and ethically than closing a decedent's estate.

Another reason courts may not effectively monitor is their unfamiliarity with the task. In most civil cases, once a case has been tried, the court's responsibilities are complete and the file is closed. Most judicial orders are self-executing, in that the court has no continuing role to carry out its orders. It is up to the individual litigants to enforce any judgment. If a victorious party needs the court's assistance in executing or enforcing a judgment, the party must come back to the court in a separate procedure to enforce the court's decree. This might be an action to garnish wages, attach real property, or request a show cause order.

The ward in a guardianship, having been found to be vulnerable, incapable of making decisions, and devoid of legal rights is rarely able to come into court to enforce the order or complain of the guardian's actions. At least one court has even questioned whether the ward had the legal capacity to contract with an attorney to challenge the guardian's actions (Miler, 1993). It is, of course, the person the court has found legally incapacitated who is the person most likely to be harmed by a guardianship order and to need further court assistance.

A common barrier to effective monitoring is lack of resources. "The burdens on courts of caseload congestion and a shortage of funds appear to have pushed the oversight responsibility of the courts further to the back of the courthouse burner. The result is ironic: as law reform tries to bring more protection to the prospective ward in the courtroom, that protection tends to vanish once the guardian has been appointed" (Regan, 1992, p. 28).

Another difficulty in writing about court monitoring of guardianship cases is the diversity among state statutes. Although 15 states have adopted the UPC or its successor, the Uniform Guardianship and Protective Procedures Act, the other states have adopted a variety of monitoring procedures. Despite the courts' reluctance to monitor guardianship cases diligently, most courts have statutory authority to do so. State legislatures have been quite receptive to include monitoring mandates in guardianship reform legislation (Regan, 1992).

MONITORING PROCESS

Periodic Reports

The primary means of monitoring is guardian self-reporting. The reports could include an inventory of all of the ward's assets, due sometime within the first two or three months after the guardian is appointed, and an accounting of receipts and disbursements provided at some point during the term of the guardianship. Thirty-nine states and the District of Columbia mandate periodic financial accountings. Ten other states make accountings discretionary with the court or only at the end of the guardianship. In the 39 states where periodic financial reporting is mandatory, the most common filing period is annually.

In 35 states, the guardians of the person must report on the personal status of their ward either annually or biennially. In 9 states, guardians need to file personal status reports only if and when the court requires it (Hurme, 1991). When a guardian has both personal and financial responsibilities, usually both reports must be filed but not necessarily simultaneously.

The content of these financial and personal status reports varies by state statute and local court practice. A financial report typically requires a fairly detailed financial statement of all receipts and disbursements during the reporting period. The general process is to start with the funds on hand at the beginning of the reporting period, add receipts, subtract disbursements, and show an ending balance. The reporting process is primarily a mathematical exercise that emphasizes accurate record keeping.

In those states that require personal status reports, 19 statutes specify what the guardian should include in the report. Guardians variously include the number and nature of contacts with the ward; purpose of the last doctor's visit; number of doctor visits or hospitalizations; social and rehabilitation services; changes in mental, physical, or emotional condition; and major decisions about, adequacy of, or changes in living arrangements. In some states, the guardian gives an opinion about the quality of care being provided if the ward is in a care facility or about the need to continue or change the guardianship (Zimny, Gilchrist, & Diamond, 1991).

Inventories and Care Plans

A common requirement in state guardianship statutes is that the guardian of the estate file an inventory of the ward's assets within the first few months after the guardian is appointed. Similar to the inventory of a decedent's estate in a probate case, the inventory in a guardianship case forces the guardian to identify and place a financial value on the ward's real and personal property. The value of the property given in the inventory also serves as the opening balance for the first accounting to the court.

A care plan is similar to a personal inventory. It establishes the starting point of the ward's social, medical, and educational needs. As with the financial inventory, it serves as the foundation by which the ward's care can be measured. As early as 1979 the American Bar Association (ABA) Commission on the Mentally Disabled recommended that the guardian develop the care plan, with the ward's participation, setting out the necessary services, means to obtain these services, and the way the guardian will exercise and share decision-making authority (American Bar Association, 1979). The main purpose of a personal care plan is to require guardians to focus on the ward's important financial and personal conditions and to make some initial decisions about how to take care of those conditions. A plan also gives the court some indication of the guardian's intentions and the opportunity to prevent shortfalls in the ward's care.

Florida's new guardianship statute contains an example of care plans. The code requires guardians to file an initial care plan 60 days after appointment. In the plan, the guardians establish how they will provide medical, mental, and personal care and social services for the ward; the best-suited residential setting; the benefits applied for; and the necessary physical and mental examinations. Guardians also attest that they have consulted with the ward and have honored the ward's wishes, if reasonable. The guardian updates the plan each year by specifying the ward's current needs and how the guardian proposes to meet those needs (Fla. Stat. Ann. § 744.362 1990).

STEPS AFTER REPORTING

Number of Cases

Despite statutory mandates in most states for guardians to report on either the financial or the personal well-being of their wards, some courts are less than diligent in implementing and enforcing these statutes. An ABA survey of local practices in guardianship monitoring indicated that many courts do little to keep track of their guardianship cases (Hurme, 1991). An earlier study by the AP found that "few state officials collect the number [of guardianship cases] from the dozens, sometimes hundreds, of probate courts within their state borders. Even courts charged with tracking guardianship cases . . . had no idea how many cases were under their jurisdiction" (Associated Press, 1987, p. 5). Obviously if a court does not know how many guardianship orders it has entered, it cannot know how well the wards under its jurisdiction are getting along.

Compliance

Not only do courts need to know how many wards are under their protection, but also they need to take steps to make sure that guardians actually file the required reports. In the 44 states that require guardian reports, the survey by Hurme (1991) revealed that only 18 states uniformly enforced the reporting requirements. In 15 other states, enforcement of reporting varied depending on the particular court. Survey respondents who practiced in one part of the state said reporting was enforced while others from different counties in the same state reported little enforcement. All survey respondents from 11 states indicated that the court did not routinely require guardians to file status reports. Although the survey included only a few counties from each state, the variation in practice from state to state and within a particular state indicates significant compliance problems. In 1991, the Cook County, Illinois, Public Guardian (Murphy, 1992, p. 86) surveyed 50 randomly selected Cook County guardianship cases initiated in 1988 and found that

- in only 2 cases were all reports filed,
- in 17 cases no accounting at all had ever been filed,
- and in 9 cases the inventory of assets, due 60 days after appointment, had never been filed.

These findings are for a state that requires accountings only once every 3 years.

Experience shows that unless courts take steps to enforce the reporting requirements, guardians will file few reports. Hurme (1991) found that those courts that routinely sent reminder notices when a report was due or overdue had higher rates of return. The Hon. Isabella Grant, Superior Court Judge, San Francisco, California, reported to the Senate Special Committee on Aging that when her court did little to enforce monitoring "we just never saw any [accountings], or if we did, it was because somebody wanted to . . . get an approval of something they had done" (Grant, 1992, p. 90). Now her court sets a time for the accounting to be on file. If it is not filed, the guardian has to come in to court and tell the judge why. Courts that enforce the reporting requirements may impose sanctions such as orders to appear in court, fines for tardy reports, or even removal of the guardian.

Examination of Reports

Effective monitoring requires more than a statutory requirement to report. Not only must the guardian file the report, but someone must review the report. A competent person should examine the personal reports and financial accountings not only for completeness and accuracy but also for the appropriateness of the guardian's expenditures and actions. Because of the inherent hazards of self-reporting by the guardian, a better practice is to require that documentary verification accompany the financial accounting statement. This should include receipts to confirm disbursements, bank statements to verify income, and broker or realtor reports to verify investment and asset value (Zimny, et al., 1991).

Ideally, the financial accounting and the personal status report should be examined simultaneously. Reviewing the two together could reveal any internal inconsistency between what is done for the ward and what is spent. For example, does the number of reported doctor visits match payments of physician charges (Zimny, et al., 1991)? A judge or other court personnel such as a magistrate, commissioner, court clerk, visitor, investigator, or even a volunteer can do this review.

Although most state statutes are silent about what happens after a guardian files a report or audit, Florida's new guardianship statute explicitly sets out the steps of court review. The court clerk has 30 days to check the initial and annual reports to see if they contain the required information and 90 days to audit the financial reports. The judge must then review the initial guardianship report within 60 days after receiving it from the clerk and the annual report within 15 days of receipt. During that review, the judge determines whether the guardian is meeting the ward's needs and acting only in the areas where the court has declared the ward incapacitated (Fla. Stat. Ann. § 774.368 - .369 1990).

Auditing

The review method and extent of court audits of accountings can take many forms. Courts generally are more comfortable reviewing accountings than personal status reports, probably because of their experience with reviewing accountings in decedents' estates. A look at three different courts illustrates the various ways audits are conducted.

Maryland

Maryland law requires each county to have a trust clerk who has substantial auditing responsibilities. The trust clerk examines the accounting to see if it is complete, verifies transactions and assets, reviews investments, and recommends any change in the bond amount. If an accounting is not satisfactory, the trust clerk can question the guardian informally or ask that the accounting be redone. More serious problems or irregularities are reported to the judge.

Minnesota

The Hennepin County, Minnesota, probate court has three staff auditors. The Minnesota code requires that the court review the files annually to verify that the accounting and personal status report are in the file and contain the required information. If any information is missing, the auditor sends the guardian a courtesy notice to file the missing information within 2 weeks. If the information is not forthcoming, the court will issue an order to file. By local court rule, the Hennepin auditors complete a full audit of all accounts every 3 years. The auditor's report is sent to the judge with a copy to the guardian and the guardian's counsel. A court referee (an assistant to the judge) then holds an in-court hearing at which the guardian answers any questions raised by the audit.

New Hampshire

The probate judge in Merrimack County, New Hampshire, holds an in-court hearing on the guardian's reports after the first year and then every other year. At these hearings, the judge requires guardians to provide all bills, receipts, and bank statements. He may look at individual bills, ask for specific canceled checks, and discuss many items on the accounting form. Interested parties receive notice of the hearing and may attend or file objections.

Court Investigators

Although a desk or paper review of the reports and accounts is a necessary monitoring component, effective monitoring requires that the court have personnel available to ferret out problems. A minimal response to a problem is for the court to issue a show cause order requiring the guardian to appear before the judge to explain a financial or care-giving action. In other instances, the court may appoint an attorney as a *guardian ad litem* to investigate a problem. A few statutes (in Maine, Michigan, Utah, Nebraska, North Dakota, Ohio, and Oregon) authorize court visitors to visit the guardian and ward if a termination or removal petition is filed or if a complaint is received. Florida courts may appoint a special master (a sort of temporary judge) to aid them in their monitoring responsibilities; Indiana judges can use the county welfare office to investigate a ward's circumstances and the guardian's conduct. Other courts, such as in Minnesota, refer problems to the Adult Protective Services office. A Kentucky court contracts for a social worker to visit wards, and a New Jersey Superior Court judge initiated a monitoring program to have court personnel telephone head nurses or administrators of nursing homes where wards were residing. The caller usually asks about the ward's general condition, if the facility had experienced any problems in dealing with the guardian, the frequency of guardian visits, and the guardian's general attentiveness to the ward/resident. For wards in private residences, the judge prevailed on the local area agency on aging to make home visits and evaluations (R. Lukens, personal communication, July 19, 1990).

Probably the most effective system to keep the court informed about a ward's well-being is found in California with its probate court investigators. Each California county has trained court staff that has responsibilities both before the guardianship hearing and after letters of appointment are granted. The court investigator visits the ward prior to the hearing, reviews the reports and audits, and also revisits each ward after the first year and then biennially. The investigator serves as the court's eyes and ears, investigating complaints, tracking missing reports or absent guardians, suggesting alternative care or recommending changes to the guardianship order. For example, the San Mateo County Court Investigator (CI) closely examines the accounting, looking for cash disbursements, reimbursements to unidentified persons, loans, gifts, speculative investments, and missing dividend entries. The CI takes the report and accounting along while visiting the ward to verify new purchases, the number of times the guardian visited the ward, and the ward's well-being. During the personal visit with the ward, the CI will examine the medical chart and meet with attending staff or family. An average review takes about three hours. By statute, the CI must determine if the ward wants to end the guardianship, if the guardianship is still needed, if the order should be changed, and if the guardian is serving the ward's best interests. After the review, the CI sends a copy of the report to the guardian and any attorney of record. The CI can also recommend that the judge order the guardian to appear in court, terminate the guardianship, appoint a successor guardian, or refer the case to the prosecutor if abuse is suspected.

Volunteer Monitors

An innovative alternative to salaried court investigators is using volunteer monitors and auditors. An important contribution to the use of volunteer monitors was made by a project conducted by the Legal Counsel for the Elderly, a department of the American Association of Retired Persons (AARP) (Legal Counsel for the Elderly, 1991). A grant from the State Justice Institute and AARP support provided the initial funding for the project. The project expanded from the original three pilot efforts in Atlanta, Houston, and

Denver to an additional three sites in Kalamazoo, San Francisco, and South Carolina (a state-wide program). Recruitment of volunteers was carried out mainly by direct mail requests to AARP members. The project focused on training volunteers to serve in three different roles, namely, as court visitors, court auditors, and records researchers (Miler & Hurme, 1991).

The volunteer court visitors go to homes to make sure wards are receiving proper care and to see whether the guardianship order needs any changes. Visitors gather information about the wards' living arrangements, social interactions, health care, mental functioning, and relationships with their guardians using a seven-page standardized form. They make only one visit unless they find a problem. They report to the court with recommendations for possible action, if any.

Volunteer auditors work with the court staff to check financial reports filed by conservators for accuracy, discrepancies, authorized expenditures, and proper investments. Using a standard review form, they rate the report and describe any problems found.

Volunteer record researchers get the court files ready for the visitors by culling old cases from the court files and determining current addresses and telephone numbers for the wards and guardians. They may find that the ward has died or moved or that the guardianship was terminated. They report their findings to the court for updating of court files. In one jurisdiction, the volunteers have access to the court computer records so they can directly enter any new information (Legal Counsel for the Elderly, 1991).

AARP has developed a 12-hour module for training volunteers that covers guardianship law and process, typical physical and mental impairments of people under guardianship, communication techniques, how to detect abuse and neglect, ethics, confidentiality, and how to use the reporting forms. Speakers include judges, Adult Protective Services staff, Area Agency on Aging staff, accountants, nurses, and ethicists (Legal Counsel for the Elderly, 1991).

Two of the jurisdictions in the original AARP project are now functioning independently, with any ongoing expenses for the volunteer program being paid by the court. Other jurisdictions have started using volunteers in various ways to assist with monitoring. For example, in Erie, Pennsylvania, visitors visit in teams of two. Volunteers do not have the entire case file for a ward but rely on a synopsis the court staff prepares. In Los Angeles, volunteer visitors supplement staff court investigators. Volunteers make the preliminary visits and refer problem cases to the staff investigators. In Connecticut, volunteer visitors visit wards in nursing homes twice monthly and report to a program coordinator (Legal Counsel for the Elderly, 1993).

As with any volunteer program, issues of recruitment, funding, supervision, and training are critical. Direct mail requests to AARP members, an existing volunteer bureau, and newspaper promotions can be used to locate volunteers. Most jurisdictions using volunteers rely on court employees to act as volunteer coordinators. The coordinator's responsibilities are usually in addition to other duties in the court. The volunteers themselves can aid in conducting the program by organizing work schedules and training sessions and by keeping program records (Legal Counsel for the Elderly, 1993). In addition to direct program costs, funds are generally required to reimburse volunteers for expenses such as mileage, parking, and long distance calls. Funds may also be required to provide liability coverage for volunteers.

Sanctions for Abuses

Whenever a possible problem within a guardianship is brought to the court's attention, the court has various options. The court may proceed informally by contacting the guardian or guardian's attorney to request additional information or by asking a government agency, such as Adult Protective Services, court visitor, or Area Agency on Aging, to make an investigation. The AARP volunteer monitoring project frequently found that to solve a problem the guardian simply needed information about community resources, help in applying for public benefits, or a referral to social services (Legal Counsel for the Elderly, 1993).

Another option is for the court to initiate formal proceedings such as a show cause order requiring guardians to appear in court to explain why the court should not take action against them. State statutes variously authorize judges to impose fines for late filings, make the guardian post bond, obtain reimbursement from the guardian's bond, change or limit the guardian's power, or remove the guardian. Especially in financial transactions, the court has the authority to set matters straight if guardians have not acted in the wards' best interests. The court may require guardians to make restitution to the wards' estate, return property or funds to the wards, or charge the guardians for unjustified losses (Perry & Hurme, 1991). Another sanction is to deny or reduce any fees or commissions the guardians request in payment for their services to wards.

The Ohio statute is an example of comprehensive sanctions. If guardians neglect or refuse to file reports when due, the court may issue a citation to compel the filing of the overdue report. If guardians do not file reports by a stated date, the court may remove the guardian, deny fees, grant a continuance, assess a penalty of $100 plus costs, or find them in contempt with a daily fine or imprisonment (Ohio Rev. Code Ann. § 2109.31(A) 1990).

Why Problems Persist

For various reasons, problems within guardianship cases may never get addressed. A problem may just never come to the court's attention. In most civil cases, it is up to one of the parties to petition the court for sanctions. In most guardianship cases, the ward is unable to bring problems to the court's attention. When a problem is presented, the court may be unequipped to make a proper investigation, reluctant to exercise oversight responsibilities, or constrained by other more pressing caseloads or fiscal pressures. Courts may be concerned that strict monitoring may increase the already severe shortage of capable guardians. "The enforcement mechanism breaks down where the only sanction open is removal of the guardian and no alternative guardian can be found" (U.S. House of Representatives, 1989, p. 13).

TYPICAL MONITORING PROBLEMS

What problems does monitoring reveal? This chapter began with three actual cases uncovered by volunteer monitors participating in the AARP National Guardianship Monitoring Program (Legal Counsel for the Elderly, 1993). That project's extensive records contain illuminating anecdotes of what can go wrong in a guardianship.

From December 1, 1990, to November 30, 1992, volunteers researched 2,582 court files, audited 3,451 annual accountings, and filed 980 reports on visits with wards. In the reports, the volunteers rated 5% of the wards to be in marginal or unacceptable circumstances and recommended that the court take some action in about 20% of these cases. A wide variety of problems were found in the ward's living arrangements, care, and finances.

The ward may not be in an appropriate living environment, as in the first example with Mrs. Thomas. The ward's condition may have deteriorated so that nursing home care is now necessary where previously home care or a board and care facility was adequate. The guardian may be unaware of alternative living facilities or reluctant to move the ward to a different environment.

The guardian may not be providing adequate health care out of either lack of knowledge or reluctance to spend the ward's money. Mr. Martin was guardian for his son who had developmental disabilities as well as a lengthy history of drug and alcohol abuse. The son had diabetes and kidney failure requiring dialysis treatments. Mr. Martin, afraid that his son would be taken away, did not take him for regularly scheduled dialysis treatments (Miler & Hurme, 1991). The volunteers also noted that the guardian may not attend to the ward's dental needs, leading to malnourishment as the ward becomes less able to chew food.

Problems relating to the ward's estate abound, not only in the AARP project but also in case law in all jurisdictions. Typical financial abuses fall frequently into two groups: guardians either are reluctant to spend money on their wards, intending to preserve the estate for heirs, or are unable to resist the temptation to use wards' money on guardians' needs. Mr. Peters' situation described at the beginning of the chapter is repeated in court after court. In one case from the AARP project, the guardian was reluctant to spend money to build a wheelchair ramp, stating that the person caring for the ward would just have to manage carrying the ward up and down the stairs when it was time to take the ward outside. A guardian, who may have little preparation for the role, may not be aware of public benefits for which the ward is eligible. Thus, the guardian may not be aware that a nursing home is inappropriately charging the ward for items covered by Medicare or Medicaid.

Family conflict also can develop into problems with a ward's care. A guardian may restrict access to the ward by other family members because of resentment or misguided attempts to "protect" the ward. Guardians who are family members may become frustrated with the extent of their responsibilities and lash out at or neglect the ward, as Mrs. Jones did. Their own health situation may deteriorate, as happened with Mrs. Thomas.

A survey conducted in 1993 of 38 Virginia Commissioners of Accounts revealed similar problems (Jaffy, 1993). Sixteen percent of the commissioners had uncovered misappropriation of funds by guardians, with an average of two such incidences per year. The commissioners further reported such problems as guardians making gifts or loans to themselves, purchasing clothes or swimming pools for themselves, using wards' funds to invest in the guardian's business or make improvements to the guardian's home, writing checks for cash, not maintaining separate accounts for the ward's funds, living rent free in the ward's home while the ward was in a nursing home, and failing to maintain records of deposits or disbursements. Zimny, et al. (1997) report a case in which a son was appointed guardian and conservator of his mother who lived in a nursing home. The son did not file the first annual accounting, and the court then found that the son lived rent free in his mother's house, used her credit cards to pay his living expenses, and paid the credit card bills with her funds.

RECOMMENDATIONS FOR IMPROVEMENT

Many courts are taking steps to address their responsibility to make certain that the purpose of guardianship is carried out by providing wards with the maximum protection of the court. They are improving the quantity and quality of supervision over guardians by enforcing reporting requirements, investigating the validity of reports of abuse or neglect, and changing orders or imposing sanctions where appropriate. Courts are becoming aware of the need to

- keep track of the whereabouts and condition of wards,
- allocate scarce resources to monitoring efforts, and
- act to correct abuses.

For some courts, just determining the number of guardianship cases on file and knowing how many wards are alive are improvements.

Monitoring efforts are on the upswing although many jurisdictions need much improvement. In most jurisdictions, the courts have sufficient statutory or equitable authority to ensure the success of the guardianship process. Difficulties in effective monitoring may be the result of lack of judicial commitment, overstrained budgets, shortage of court staffing and community resources, or less than zealous advocacy on the wards' behalf.

Needed: A Comprehensive Process

Effective monitoring has many components. Although requiring annual reports on the financial and personal well-being of the ward is critical, this is only one segment of a comprehensive monitoring process. The process also must include determining what is the most significant information the court needs. Due to the inherent limitations of self-reporting by the guardian, the report should be designed to encourage narrative responses that provide the reviewer with an explanation of the ward's circumstances, the care provided, and the need to continue or change the guardianship.

An additional monitoring component is for the courts to encourage and enforce the filing requirement. Courts need to set up filing or tickler systems so they know when reports are due or late and send reminder notices if guardians do not file reports on time.

Because guardians' responsibilities can be extensive and difficult, the court should take steps to instruct guardians on how to carry out responsibilities, including instruction on locating community resources to assist in the ward's care, filing reports, and managing financial accounts. The court can do this through written instructions, training sessions, and videotapes. The guardian's task could be simplified if the court assembles a packet with

- a statement of guardian duties and responsibilities,
- a timetable of all reporting dates,
- sample forms,
- examples of sanctions, and
- names and phone numbers of court support staff (Zimny, et al., 1991).

A report tucked away in a dusty court folder does the ward little good. Someone needs to examine the report, not only for completeness but also for appropriateness. Court examiners need to know what they are to look for and what to do if a problem develops. The court needs to have access to persons who not only can investigate problems but also can periodically visit wards to verify their guardian's care report. The use of volunteer monitors helps stretch scarce resources to provide additional hands, eyes, and ears for the court.

Just like all of us, a ward's needs, circumstances, or level of capacity may change. The care of a ward is an ongoing process, so the court should periodically review the need to continue or change the guardianship order. This can be done as part of the annual review process or in a specific continuation hearing. All participants in the guardianship process should be alert for ways to increase the ward's autonomy and restore as many civil rights and decision-making responsibilities as the ward's abilities allow.

As more courts recognize the special nature of the guardianship process and focus more on the purpose and outcome, more judicial commitment to guardianship monitoring should ensue. A guardianship case does not end with the entry of an order. Rather the entry of the order is just the beginning of an ongoing judicial responsibility to make certain that the protective purpose of the guardianship proceeding is being fulfilled.

SUMMARY

To carry out the protective purpose of guardianship, the court must monitor the performance of the guardians it appoints to care for wards. All manner of abuse and neglect of a ward's person and finances can and do occur. Monitoring ordinarily involves reports on the person and the finances of wards prepared by the guardians *and* reviewed by the court. Court investigators, paid or volunteers, add greatly to monitoring effectiveness.

REFERENCES

American Bar Association. (1979). *Guardianship & Conservatorship*. Washington, DC: Author.

Associated Press. (1987). *Guardians of the elderly: An ailing system. A special report*.

Averill, L. H., Jr. (1978). *Uniform Probate Code in a nutshell*. St. Paul, MN: West Publishing.

Fla. Stat. Ann. § 744.362 (West Supp. 1990).

Fla. Stat. Ann. § 774.368 - .369 (West Supp. 1990).

Grant, I. (1992). Roundtable discussion on guardianship, *Workshop before the Special Committee on Aging*, United States Senate, 102d Congress, 2d Session (June 2, 1992) (Senate Hearing 102-820, Serial No. 102-22).

Hurme, S. (1991). *Steps to enhance guardianship monitoring*. Washington, DC: American Bar Association.

Jaffy, L. (1993). *Survey of Virginia Commissioners of Accounts on guardians for the incapacitated*. (based on questionnaire issued by David C. Dorset, Commissioner of Accounts for Henrico County). Washington, DC: American Bar Association. (Survey results on file with chapter author).

Keilitz, I. (1992). Roundtable discussion on guardianship, *Workshop before the Special Committee on Aging*, United States Senate, 102d Congress, 2d Session (June 2, 1992) (Senate Hearing 102-820, Serial No. 102-22).

Kindregan, C. P. (1979). The California crawl: Reforming probate administration in California. *Santa Clara Law Review, 19,* (citing Wellman, R. V. (1969). The Uniform Probate Code: A possible answer to probate avoidance. *Indiana Law Journal, 44,* page 191).

Law v. John Hanson Savings & Loan, 400 A.2d 1154, 1158 (Md. Ct. Spec. App. 1979).

Legal Counsel for the Elderly. (1991). *AARP volunteers: A resource for strengthening guardianships, final report to the State Justice Institute.* Washington, DC: Author.

Legal Counsel for the Elderly. (1993). *AARP volunteers: A resource for strengthening guardianships, second final report to the State Justice Institute.* Washington, DC: Author.

Miler, S. & Hurme, S. (1991). Guardianship monitoring: An advocate's role. *Clearinghouse Review, 25,* 654–661.

Miler, S. (1993). National guardianship monitoring program can be resource for courts, in Innovative approaches to guardianship, *Workshop before the Special Committee on Aging,* United States Senate, 103d Congress, 1st Session (April 16, 1993 (Senate Hearing 103-155, Serial No. 102-22).

Murphy, P. T. (1992). Roundtable discussion on guardianship, *Workshop before the Special Committee on Aging,* United States Senate, 102d Congress, 2d Session (June 2, 1992) (Senate Hearing 102-820, Serial No. 102-22).

National Conference of Commissioners on Uniform State Laws. (1987). Uniform Probate Code § 3-101. *Uniform Laws Annotated, 8,* 221.

Ohio Rev. Code Ann. § 2109.31(A) (Anderson 1990).

Perry, J. & Hurme, S. (1991). Guardianship monitoring and enforcement nationwide. *Mental and Physical Disability Law Reporter, 15,* 304–309.

Regan, J. (1992). Roundtable discussion on guardianship, *Workshop before the Special Committee on Aging,* United States Senate, 102d Congress, 2d Session (June 2, 1992) (Senate Hearing 102-820, Serial No. 102-22).

Uniform Probate Code. (1987). Art. III, General Comment.

United States House of Representatives, Select Committee on Aging. (1989). *Model standards to ensure quality guardianship and representative payeeship services,* Committee Publication No. 101-729.

Zimny, G., Gilchrist, B., & Diamond, J. (1991). *A national model for judicial review of guardians' performance: Final report.* St. Louis: St. Louis University. (Includes sample accounting and personal status reports).

Zimny, G., Diamond, J., Mau, M., Law, A., & Chung, C. (1997). Six-year longitudinal study of finances of elderly wards under guardianship. *The Journal of Ethics, Law, and Aging, 3(2),* 91–101.

PART 4

Research

CHAPTER 10

Empirical Research on Guardianship

George H. Zimny

As indicated in part by the preceding chapters in this book, guardianship is an extremely important, complex, expensive, widespread, and evolving activity that involves and affects many different people. Given these characteristics, it is not surprising that a rather large body of information about guardianship exists. A substantial amount of that information is based on legal research, but over the past several decades the amount of information about guardianship based on empirical research studies has increased substantially. One reason for the increase is that greater numbers of social scientists such as psychologists, sociologists, and gerontologists became interested in guardianship, a topic that had ordinarily been perceived as belonging in the legal and judicial domains. Another reason is that the research studies are often focused on practical problems encountered in guardianship, and the findings can produce a better understanding of the nature and cause of problems and can contribute to the resolution of problems.

Later in this chapter, some of the "Calls for Research" that have been made in the guardianship literature will be examined as a way of illustrating the type and range of research questions that can be investigated empirically. Some of the difficulties in conducting empirical research on guardianship questions will also be presented. First, though, let us briefly review an example of a problem-oriented empirical research study of guardianship.

AN EXAMPLE

Although empirical research studies have been cited in previous chapters, usually just one or two of the major findings are noted. To provide a more complete example, a recent study is described below that dealt with a current guardianship problem that will increase in severity during the coming decades. The study was conceived, designed, and carried out by Zimny and Diamond (1994) with grant support provided by the AARP Andrus Foundation. The title was *Social Service Agencies as Guardians of Elderly Wards*.

Problem

As the number of elderly persons, especially the old old (over 85), increases drastically over the coming decades, the number of guardianships of the elderly will increase. Who will serve as guardians? The usual sources of guardians are family members and friends, public guardians, and in recent years private professional guardianship companies. Each of these sources has advantages but also distinct disadvantages. For example, women family members, mainly daughters and nieces, are often guardians, but increasing numbers of them are in the workforce and some of them are themselves elderly. Examples of abuse by private professional guardians were cited in chapter 8.

What about social service agencies serving as guardians of elderly wards? Many agencies have professional staff members who are experienced in dealing with elderly persons, have contacts with many different resources for help and services, and have a tradition of support and concern for those in need. A review of the existing literature turned up virtually no information about social service agencies as guardians of elderly wards.

Research Questions

Two questions requiring empirical investigation thus arose. First, what social service agencies in our country are now serving as guardians of elderly wards? The answer to that question could result in publication of a directory listing the agencies, thus making the guardianship services of the agencies more widely known and, hopefully, more widely utilized. Second, how do social service agencies go about serving as guardians of elderly wards? Detailed information obtained in answer to that question could serve to help social service agencies begin to provide guardianship services and could help other agencies improve their guardianship services.

Method

Panels

Two panels were established at the outset of the project to serve as expert resources to the project staff throughout the project. The consultation panel was composed of a judge, attorney, and a social service agency director. The evaluation panel consisted of four persons, each of whom was a staff member at a different social service agency providing guardianship services.

Survey

In order to answer the first question dealing with social service agencies that were serving as guardians of elderly wards, a national survey was conducted with the cooperation of four national social service agency umbrella organizations. They were the Association of Jewish Family and Children's Agencies, Catholic Charities USA, Evangelical Lutheran Church in America, and Family Service America. The survey forms and cover letter were drafted by the project staff, reviewed by the panel members, and finalized by the project staff. The survey sought to determine, first, the number and characteristics of social service agencies that were currently serving as guardians for elderly wards and, second, the number of agencies that were not providing that service and why not. Using mailing labels provided by the umbrella organizations, the survey was sent to 496 agencies throughout the country.

Visits

The second question dealt with how social service agencies provide guardianship services to elderly wards. To answer this question, eight social service agencies providing such services, two from each umbrella organization, were visited by the project's two investigators. Since information about how such services were provided at agencies had never been obtained before, a great deal of revision and consultation went into the preparation of the interview protocol to be used by the investigators during each visit. Information was obtained about 15 areas, including number and characteristics of elderly wards, guardianship of the person, conservatorship of the estate, procedures for handling wards' estates, liability, sources of income for the guardianship service, and volunteers. Prior to the visit to each of the eight agencies, the agency director gave permission for the visit to be made, each staff member willing to be interviewed signed a consent form, and travel times and interview appointments were scheduled. Each visit lasted two to four days, all consenting staff members involved in providing guardianship services were interviewed by two investigators together, and all interviews were audiotaped (with the permission of each interviewee).

Results

Survey

A completed survey was returned by 359 (72%) of the 496 agencies surveyed. Of the 359 agencies, 52 (14%) stated that they provided guardianship services. Three of the 52 agencies did not provide guardianship services for elderly wards, and 43 of the remaining 49 agencies indicated on the survey form that they would be willing to be included in a directory of social service agencies providing guardianship services for elderly wards. The three main reasons given for not providing guardianship services were the service is provided elsewhere, guardianship is not part of the agency's mission, and staff inadequacies.

Visits

The eight agencies visited by the investigators varied in many respects. The number of elderly wards ranged from 11 to 118, and the total value of the wards' estates in an agency ranged from $44,000 to $18,776,000. A staff member was appointed personally as guardian of the person in one agency, but in the other seven the agency was appointed guardian. The agency was appointed conservator in all eight agencies. The use of computers in handling wards' finances ranged from no use to use of a sophisticated computer system. The sources of income for the guardianship programs ranged from one source, usually a contract, to many sources. One agency had 60 volunteers; most had none. The most striking similarity among the eight agencies was the professionalism, expertise, concern, and dedication of the staff members providing guardianship services for elderly wards under often very difficult circumstances.

Reports and Dissemination

Several reports were prepared for dissemination to different groups and individuals. A full report was prepared that described the entire project. The report included a listing of the 43 agencies providing guardianship services for elderly wards. The major portion of the report was a detailed description of the findings for the 15 areas in each of the 8 agencies visited.

Two other reports were prepared. One report contained a brief description of the project plus detailed descriptions of the findings of the visits to each of the eight agencies arranged by the area for which information was sought during the visits. For example, the area of liability contained a description of how each of the eight agencies dealt with the issue of liability of the agency and its staff members in providing guardianship services. As another example, the report contained eight descriptions of the often complicated procedures used by agencies in handling and protecting the financial assets of wards. The other report was a directory of the 43 agencies providing guardianship service for elderly wards.

A copy of the full report was sent to various groups and individuals such as the four umbrella organizations. Copies of the other two reports were sent to the 496 agencies. In addition, as awareness of the project increased throughout the country, due to presentations at professional meetings and to articles in various newsletters, requests for reports of the project were received.

RESEARCH DIFFICULTIES

Empirical research on guardianship is subject to the same basic requirements, difficulties, and limitations as empirical research on any topic. In addition, guardianship presents its special difficulties with respect to certain aspects of conducting empirical research. One special difficulty is considered here, namely, generalization of research findings. This difficulty is not unique to studies of guardianship but is one that is enhanced by the factors involved in guardianship.

Generalization

Empirical research studies on guardianship, as on any topic, are ordinarily carried out using samples of some population with the intent of applying the findings not just to the particular members of the sample but to the broader population from which the sample was drawn and which the sample was to represent. This process of generalizing findings from samples to populations constitutes a very serious problem in guardianship research because of the variability that exists in factors involved in guardianship. Four such factors are cited below.

One, the guardianship statute is different in each of the 50 states and the District of Columbia, so a research finding obtained in one state may not be very relevant or even possible in another state.

Two, within a given state, there are many courts, usually probate courts, that hear guardianship cases. In Missouri, there are 115. These courts differ in many ways, such as rural-urban, volume of cases, percentage of indigent wards, and size of staff. As a result, the findings obtained in a study of one court in a state will apply in only varying degrees to other courts in the same state.

Three, each court within a state has a different judge. Judges have wide leeway in determining the specific manner in which they will carry out statutory provisions in their own courts. Thus, the findings of a study in a rural low-volume court in a state may not be directly applicable to another rural low-volume court in the same state because of differences in the judges.

Four, courts within a state and in different states can vary widely with respect to guardians. Guardians can differ in many ways, such as in age, sex, occupation, honesty, greed, and relationship to wards. For example, prior to 1993, the statute in Missouri did not allow appointment of an agency as guardian of the person, so any study of agencies as guardians conducted before 1993 would have had no relevance to guardians in Missouri.

The result of this variability in statutes, courts, judges, guardians, and still other factors is that generalizing the results of studies of guardianship is a very difficult problem. Some specific examples of the difficulty are provided by two of the studies frequently cited in the previous chapter on court monitoring of guardianships. In each study (Hurme, 1991; Zimny, et al., 1991), visits were made by the investigator to six courts in different states in order to describe the staff and procedures used by each court to monitor the performance of guardians and conservators.

These two studies cost hundreds of thousands of dollars and took 12 to 18 months to complete. Even so, they investigated courts in only 12 of 50 states and only one court out of the many in each state. If the courts within a state were similar and if the guardianship practices of each state were similar, then findings from 12 courts in 12 different states might be safely generalized to other courts in a state and to other states.

The lack of similarity within and between states is demonstrated by statements made in the report of each study, however. "The judge from a rural Kansas county sees no need for an investigator, while one of his colleagues from a metropolitan Kansas county finds a critical need for one" (Hurme, 1991, pp. 77–78). "In one court, for example, guardianship records had to be obtained through the computer located in the capital city while in another court the records were stored in the court's computer" (Zimny, et al., 1991, p. 41). "Once accounts and reports are received each court has different review procedures" (Hurme, 1991, p. 77). "Each of the six courts had developed specific detailed procedures and materials that were to be employed by its staff in executing monitoring actions" (Zimny, et al., 1991, p. 41).

Except for the development of national guardianship laws, there is little that can be done about the difficulties inherent in generalizing the findings of guardianship studies. Research on guardianship must be carried out, but overgeneralization of findings must be avoided by both investigators who write reports of studies and those who read the study reports.

CALLS FOR RESEARCH

As noted at the beginning of this chapter, guardianship is an extremely complex activity. As such, it contains many questions and topics that are subject to empirical investigation. One indication of the variety of questions that have been studied empirically is given by the empirical research studies cited throughout this book.

Out of the many possible, what are the questions or problems in guardianship that should be investigated empirically? There is no one answer to the question, of course, and answers will differ from person to person and from time to time. One way to provide some representative answers to the question, however, is by examining "Calls for Research" that have been issued at various times by individuals and organizations interested in guardianship.

Three quite different "calls" are described below. The first is contained in a congressional report, the second in an editorial, and the third in the report of an extensive national study.

1989: Select Committee on Aging, House of Representatives

One of the publications resulting from congressional investigations of guardianship and other surrogate management arrangements was a report by Congressman James Florio, Chairman of the Subcommittee on Housing and Consumer Interests, Select Committee on Aging, U. S. House of Representatives. Included in the report was a section dealing with research.

> A great deal of research is needed on both the imposition and the provision of guardianship and representative payeeship services in this country. In writing this report, the authors were forced to make numerous assumptions about trends in surrogate decisionmaking based on general demographic data and anecdotal evidence. There is a serious need for a broad range of statistical data and descriptive information on which to base policy and program development (U.S. House of Representatives, 1989, pp. 29–30).

Six broad areas of research were then listed, often with identification of more specific topics within an area. The initial statement in each of the six areas is presented below, and the listing of specific research topics is given for the first area as an example.

> (1) Research about the guardianship and representative payee process (the process for imposing these mechanisms as well as for monitoring them once imposed), and the effect of laws and regulations upon that process. This would include research on the quality and timeliness of notice to the proposed ward; the length of the hearing; the presence of counsel; the evidence and standard of proof used by the court; the presence of the proposed ward at the hearing; the extent of authority granted to the guardian; the completeness of files and reports required to be filed with the courts; and so forth . . . .
> (2) Research about the numbers and characteristics of adults affected by guardianship and representative payeeship . . . .
> (3) Research about the nature of guardianships and representative payeeships and their impact upon individuals . . . .
> (4) Research on factors that "trigger" the filing of petitions for guardianship in an attempt to identify services and assistance that might divert some

individuals from guardianship if such assistance and services were available and utilized.

(5) Research on the providers of guardianship and representative payee services—who are they, how are they related to their wards, what are their characteristics? . . .

(6) Research on the availability, utilization, and effectiveness of alternatives such as money management, durable powers of attorney, living wills, and so forth (U.S. House of Representatives, 1989, pp. 30–31).

1991: New Directions for Guardianship Research

In an editorial in *The Gerontologist*, Iris (1991) identified a number of directions in which she believes guardianship research should begin to move. Three such directions involving subject populations and research methodology are described below.

Efforts to define the guardianship system, reform it, and provide reasonable alternatives to this most restrictive protection must now recognize all populations of persons with incapacities served by this one system. Researchers must expand their focus by engaging in comparative studies across disability types and age groups. Such comparative research can tell us much about how the guardianship system functions in its totality, and highlight the need for system-wide change. Focusing exclusively on guardianship for the elderly diverts us from seeing both the commonalities and differences across populations served by the same guardianship system.

Representatives of various population subgroups within the guardianship system remains to be addressed. We know that not all older people who become incapacitated end up with guardians, nor do all persons with mental retardation receive a guardian at their eighteenth birthday. Yet, why not? What factors enable some individuals to stay outside the system and what factors bring them in? These are currently unanswerable questions, given the state of our existing database. To answer them, guardianship research needs to look beyond the domain of guardianship itself, using a comparative, and more qualitative methodology.

We must also look more intensively at what happens to wards once they are in the guardianship system. Much of the current knowledge about guardianship is based on examinations of petitions filed (Bulcroft, Kielkopf, & Tripp, 1991; Iris, 1989). Yet we know little about what happens to people as they age within the system. A more longitudinal view of guardianship, beginning with an examination of ongoing cases as well as new petitions needs to be developed (Iris, 1991, pp. 148–149).

1994: Areas of Further Research

The National Study of Guardianship Systems was conducted by The Center for Social Gerontology (1994) with Penelope Hommel as project director. This study constitutes a good example of an effort to cope with the problem of generalization described earlier in this chapter. The study "examined guardianship practices in over 700 cases for guardianship of persons 60 years of age or older, in 30 jurisdictions in 10 states" (The Center for Social Gerontology, 1994, p. 1). Based on the extensive experiences and findings of this study, a series of 16 "Areas of Further Research" were identified. The statement of each area was followed by specific research questions that could be investigated. One example of specific questions is given (for number 2) among the 16 areas listed below (The Center for Social Gerontology, 1994, p. 5).

1. Relationship between race and gender and guardianship.
2. Effect of respondents' financial resources on the guardianship process.

Our profile of parties revealed a wide range of estate values among respondents, leaving still unanswered speculation about the role that the respondent's financial resources play in the decision to file a petition and in the court's decision to grant or deny guardianship. More focused research is needed on such questions as: Does wealth put you at greater risk of conservatorship, or do wealthy people have financial advisors who assist in setting up trusts prior to incapacity and thereby avoid conservatorship? Do relatives and social service agencies have a greater concern for preserving and controlling the estate of the person of modest income and assets because every penny of their funds is crucial to their maintenance? Does the difficulty of obtaining funds for the care of lower income elders increase the probability of conservatorship for them? Does wealth make any difference at all in whether or not an individual ends up in the guardianship system? Do different socio-economic groups fare differently once in the system?

3. Effectiveness of advance planning and use of alternatives to guardianship.
4. Barriers to respondents' attendance at the hearing and the effect of respondents' presence on proceedings and outcomes.
5. Need for and effectiveness of legal representation of respondents.
6. Role of attorneys for petitioners.
7. Role played by investigators/guardians ad litem and analysis of their reports to the court.
8. Role of medical evidence and analysis of contents of medical reports.

9. Contents of functional assessment instruments and protocols.
10. Contested guardianship cases.
11. Effect of guardianship proceedings and guardianship appointment on petitioners and respondents.
12. Role of agencies in the guardianship system.
13. Nature of the association between nursing home placement and guardianship.
14. Judicial attitudes to guardianship reform.
15. Effects of legislative initiatives on guardianship.
16. Effects of societal and demographic changes on guardianship.

GUARDIANSHIP REFORM AND RESEARCH

Reform

Given the importance, complexity, and variability of guardianship in our country, it is not surprising that calls have been made to reform and improve the process by making changes both in state guardianship statutes and in the ways judges conduct guardianship cases (see Revisions and Reforms in chapter 2). Some calls are made by national bodies convened for the expressed purpose of generating recommendations to improve the process, as in the example of the National Guardianship Symposium (The Wingspread Conference) discussed next. Other calls are made by research studies whose findings serve as the basis for recommendations for improving particular aspects of the guardianship process. Examples of these research recommendations are given below.

The Wingspread Conference

A major national call for reform was made by the Wingspread Conference (Coleman & Dooley, 1990; Brown, 1988). Brown (1988) described the conference purpose and participants.

The Symposium was designed to develop practical recommendations to assist states improve their guardianship systems by providing the basis for amendments to guardianship laws and practices. Forty symposium participants came from 20 states and included judges, court administrators, practicing attorneys, scholars from law, medicine, and the social sciences, guardianship agency directors, and other participants in the guardianship system (p. 5).

Recommendations were made in six areas, namely, due process, defining incapacity, judicial practices, accountability of guardians, guardianship agencies, and overview. Research was included among the recommendations. "The Symposium called for detailed research regarding guardianship and alternatives so that further reforms can be developed and court and guardian performance can be assessed" (Brown, 1988, p. 6). This recommendation by the conference explicitly recognizes that detailed, presumably empirical, research can lead to the development of reforms in guardianship and thus contribute to the improvement of the process. Research can indeed make such a contribution as shown by the examples which follow.

Research

Research studies focus on fairly specific questions or problems, and recommendations generated by the studies tend to be more focused than those produced by national conferences. The research recommendations are based on data collected in the studies, although they do represent the interpretation and application of the study findings by the investigators.

The two research studies on monitoring of guardians' performance (Hurme, 1991; Zimny, et al., 1991) cited earlier in this chapter and in the previous chapter provide excellent examples of research recommendations. Hurme (1991) generated 10 recommendations, one of which is given below.

IV. Courts can enforce the statutory reporting requirements by

- Establishing computer or tickler systems so the court knows when the guardian's personal status reports and accountings are due or are late;
- Notifying the guardian promptly when a personal status report or accounting is not filed on time;
- Entering a show cause order if the guardian has not responded promptly to the notice to file;
- Routinely imposing monetary penalties for late filings of personal status reports or accountings, payable from the guardian's funds;
- Sending the state bar grievance committee a copy of any delinquency notice sent to an attorney who serves as a guardian (p. 31).

Each of the five points in the recommendation was discussed in the report, and examples of procedures, more specific suggestions, and findings from court visits were given. "The arrival of the sheriff at the guardian's door with a notice to show cause is an effective way to demonstrate that the court expects reports and accounts to be filed" (Hurme, 1991, p. 33).

Zimny, et al. (1991) generated 15 recommendations. One states that "The personal reports and accounts together are thoroughly audited and a sample of major items in each is verified" (p. 10). In the discussion of this recommendation, it was suggested that the personal report on the ward and the financial accounting be audited together by the same court staff member so that items in each can be cross-checked with each other. It was also suggested that a sample of major items in the personal report and in the financial account be verified by a telephone call or a letter. "Physician visits [noted in the personal report] could be checked not only by looking for charges in the account but also by calling or writing the physician's office for verification of the visit" (p. 11).

Future Reforms

Guardianship reform does take place. Wood (1992) describes changes in state guardianship laws that were made in eight states during the period of May through August of 1992, including the massive reform of the law in New York.

Reforms must continue to be made in the future. The complexity of the guardianship process provides a vast array of aspects to change and problems to solve. Guardianship is becoming increasingly important due to the aging of our population. Calls for reform will continue from individuals and organizations in each state, from national bodies, and from research findings and researchers. The response to these calls will be changes that will help the guardianship process in our country to better achieve its purpose of protecting those who are unable to protect themselves.

SUMMARY

Guardianship is an extremely complex process, and many of the questions and problems present in guardianship are amenable to empirical investigation. Various calls for more guardianship research provide concrete examples of what can and should be investigated. Research findings provide an empirical basis for recommendations leading to guardianship reform.

REFERENCES

Brown, R. N. (1988, Fall). National symposium recommendations to improve the guardianship system. *Bifocal, 9*(3), 1, 5–7.

Bulcroft, K., Kielkopf, M. R., & Tripp, K. (1991). *Elderly wards and their legal guardians: Analysis of county probate records in Ohio and Washington. The Gerontologist, 31,* 156–164.

Coleman, N., & Dooley, J. (1990). Making the guardianship system work. *Generations,* Supplement, 47–50.

Hurme, S. B. (1991). *Steps to enhance guardianship monitoring.* Washington, DC: American Bar Association.

Iris, M. (1989). *Implementation of the disabled adults statute in Illinois: A survey and analysis of the 1985 docket and court records in Cook, Lake and DuPage counties.* Final Report. Metropolitan Chicago Coalition on Aging. Chicago, Illinois.

Iris, M. A. (1991). New directions for guardianship research (Editorial). *The Gerontologist, 31*(2), 148–149.

The Center for Social Gerontology. (1994). *National study of guardianship systems: Implications for additional research.* Ann Arbor, MI: Author.

United States House of Representatives, Select Committee on Aging. (1989). *Model standards to ensure quality guardianship and representative payeeship services,* Committee Publication No. 101-729.

Wood, E. (1992, September/October). State guardianship legislation: Directions of reform. *Elder Law Forum, 4*(5), 17–19.

Zimny, G. H. & Diamond, J. A. (1994). *Social service agencies as guardians of elderly wards: Final report.* St. Louis: St. Louis University.

Zimny, G. H., Gilchrist, B. J., & Diamond, J. A. (1991). *A national model for judicial review of guardians' performance.* St. Louis: Saint Louis University.

Index

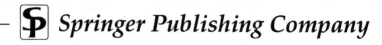

Elder Abuse and Neglect, 2nd Edition
Causes, Diagnosis, and Intervention Strategies

Mary Joy Quinn, RN, MA
Susan K. Tomita, MSW, PhD

"...the model developed by Quinn and Tomita is especially important in guiding practitioners and planners toward effective detection, assessment and intervention with this population. In addition, their model is well-grounded in the literature and represents a scholarly, as well as practical, achievement." —**Patricia J. Brownell,** DSW,
Fordham University, Graduate School of Social Service

In this new edition of their classic volume, the authors present their comprehensive model of detection, assessment, and intervention for elder abuse and neglect. The authors examine the nature and types of mistreatment including physical, sexual, psychological, and financial abuse. Through their important Elder Abuse Diagnosis and Intervention Model (EADI), systematic and realistic interventions are provided for each type of abuse.

The volume concludes with information on legal interventions with suggestions on how the practitioner should act in the courtroom, give testimony, document findings, and prepare for legal involvement with the criminal justice system. Actual legal tools are located in the appendix.

Contents:

Springer Series on Social Work
1997   384pp   0-8261-5122-1   softcover

536 Broadway, New York, NY 10012-3955 • (212) 431-4370 • Fax (212) 941-7842